Vegas Born

The Remarkable Story of The Golden Knights

Steve Carp

BookLocker

Published by BookLocker.com, Inc., St. Petersburg, Florida.

Printed on acid-free paper.

BookLocker.com, Inc.
2018

First Edition

Dedication

In memory of my dad, Joel Carp, who turned me on to hockey and would have loved the Golden Knights.

CONTENTS

Prologue

The Stanley Cup stands 35 and one-quarter inches tall and weighs 34 and a half pounds. And when Alex Ovechkin accepted the trophy from NHL commissioner Gary Bettman shortly after 8 p.m. on June 7, 2018, at T-Mobile Arena in Las Vegas, Nevada, it signaled the end of the Washington Capitals' decades of futility and frustration.

As Ovechkin picked up the Cup and held it over his head, he admitted it was a little heavier than he expected it to be. But as he lifted the silver chalice, he also lifted the cloud from the franchise which had drafted him in 2006 as the NHL's number one draft pick.

George McPhee, the man responsible for drafting Ovechkin, wasn't watching. He was in no mood to be happy for Ovechkin or the other 11 Capitals who would skate around the rink with the Cup, players he had drafted or traded for or signed as free agents during his 17-year tenure as Washington's general manager.

McPhee was very proud of his most recent accomplishment, that being the building of the most successful expansion franchise in professional sports history.

The Vegas Golden Knights had set all sorts of records en route to the Stanley Cup Final. They had won 51 games. They had amassed 109 points. They won the Pacific Division title.

They were Western Conference champions, having defeated the Los Angeles Kings, the San Jose Sharks and the Winnipeg Jets in consecutive playoff series to get there.

And they were three games from winning the Stanley Cup. They defeated the Capitals 6-4 in Game 1 and it appeared they were going to culminate their improbable journey with a championship. Plans were even being made for a parade down Las Vegas Boulevard, better known to Las Vegans as the Strip, though the team distanced itself from any parade talk.

But the Capitals proved to be a formidable opponent. Coach Barry Trotz made a few adjustments and they would win the next four games, shutting down the Golden Knights' explosive offense.

Yes, the Capitals managed to catch some breaks over those four games. Goaltender Braden Holtby made an unbelievable save with two minutes to play in Game 2 on Alex Tuch to keep the Capitals in front as Washington would go on to win 3-2 and even the series at a game apiece.

In Game 4, with the Knights trailing two games to one, James Neal had an open net in the first period and appeared to be ready to put his team ahead. Instead, Neal's shot clanged off the left goalpost and the Capitals would go on to score four unanswered goals and put a stranglehold on the series with a three games to one lead.

And as resilient as the Golden Knights were, the Capitals were equally resilient. They came back from a 3-2 deficit in the third period on goals from Devante Smith-Pelly and Lars Eller, then turned it over to their goaltender to close the door.

As the final horn sounded, the Knights skated to their goaltender, Marc-Andre Fleury, to embrace him and thank him for what he did to give them a chance to play for the Stanley

Cup. Fleury had three rings from his time with the Pittsburgh Penguins and going into the Stanley Cup Final he had been nothing short of sensational. He was considered the favorite to win the Conn Smythe Trophy, which goes to the Most Valuable Player in the playoffs.

That honor would ultimately go to Ovechkin.

As the players lined up for the traditional handshakes, they were greeted by a long standing ovation by the Golden Knights' fans. It was tough to have come this far only to fall short. But as center Pierre-Edouard Bellemare said, "Only one team gets to go home happy at the end of the season."

There was hockey in Las Vegas long before the Golden Knights arrived. The sport has roots dating back to the 1960s when the semipro Las Vegas Gamblers played at the old Commercial Center rink off East Sahara Avenue. There was also the Outlaws, another independent semipro team.

In 1993, the city welcomed the Las Vegas Thunder, which played in the International Hockey League, which had grown from a midwestern bus league to one that stretched to the West Coast and was looking to challenge the American Hockey League as the game's Triple-A level. The Thunder, which was coached by former New York Islanders star Butch Goring and built by longtime hockey executive Bob Strumm, won their division in their inaugural season and would sign several familiar names. Radek Bonk played for the Thunder. So did Alexei Yashin. Curtis Joseph, Clint Malarchuk, Pokey Reddick, Ruslan Salei and Petr Nedved all wore the Thunder sweater either before, during or after their NHL careers.

Despite having regular success on the ice, the Thunder folded in 1999 after they failed to secure an extension on their lease with the Thomas & Mack Center. Hockey returned to the city in 2003 when the Las Vegas Wranglers of the ECHL came to town and played their home games at the Orleans Arena. The Wranglers were initially coached by Glen Gulutzan, who would eventually go on to be an NHL head coach, first in Dallas, then in Calgary. The team had a winning record in nine of its 11 seasons and went to the Kelly Cup Final in 2008.

The ECHL was the equivalent of double-A hockey and it was affordable. Billy Johnson, the team's president, had a free hand to promote and the team drew good crowds, particularly on weekends. The Wranglers would send 19 players to the NHL, one of whom happened to be Deryk Engelland.

But like the Thunder, the Wranglers were having lease issues. And when their lease was up in 2014, the Boyd Group, which owned the Orleans and operated the Orleans Arena, decided it didn't want an anchor tenant. The team suspended operations and folded by late 2015.

Many of those Wranglers fans were starving for hockey. And even though the NHL meant higher prices than what they were used to paying, they embraced the Golden Knights. Not only did they have a team to root for again, they had a team playing at the game's highest level. It was a team that would provide countless thrills and a lifetime of memories in its inaugural season.

It had been a truly remarkable run, one no one in their right mind could have predicted. Before the season, few predicted the team would even post a winning record, much less make the playoffs. Those that did take an optimistic point of view and thought this team of "Golden Misfits," as the players called themselves jokingly, probably weren't convinced they would win a single playoff series, much less three. The players had been cast aside by their former teams and James Neal, who was left exposed in the NHL Expansion Draft by the Nashville Predators, said the Knights were a bunch of golden misfits.

But this team exceeded everyone's expectations, including that of its owner, Bill Foley, who was hoping to make the playoffs by the third season and compete for the Stanley Cup in six. The timetable had been moved up and nobody was complaining.

And as the Capitals prepared to receive the Stanley Cup from NHL commissioner Gary Bettman and really start celebrating, the Golden Knights' players gathered near center ice and raised their sticks in a salute to their fans.

The cheers grew even louder, and as Bettman appeared on the ice to present the Cup to the Capitals, he was roundly booed.

"You guys have proved you're a real NHL city," he said jokingly.

Real indeed.

1. The Unlikeliest Of Partners

On May 13, 2013, the Maloof Family completed the sale of the Sacramento Kings to a consortium led by Vivek Ranadive for $534 million. At the time, it was the largest price paid for an NBA team.

The Maloofs were sports nuts. They loved being owners. Back in the late 1970s the family owned the Houston Rockets. Eventually, they would sell the team to Charlie Thomas, a Houston car dealer, for $11 million in 1982.

In 1999 the family got back in the basketball business, this time in Sacramento. They had launched a successful business venture in Las Vegas, opening the Fiesta Hotel and Casino on North Rancho Drive and it had proved to be a huge success. It was a neighborhood joint where locals could gamble, eat, drink and not have to go down to the Las Vegas Strip.

At about the same time the family was getting back into sports, it was breaking ground on The Palms, an upscale hotel and casino on West Flamingo Road, a mile and a half from the Strip. The land was cheap, the location ideal and with their prior success with the Fiesta, which the Maloofs had sold to the Station Casinos Corporation — another company dedicated to catering to locals — things were quickly falling into place for the family.

The NBA welcomed the Maloofs back as brothers Joe and Gavin took control of the team.

Meanwhile, George Maloof oversaw the construction and, ultimately, the running of the Palms. Both ventures were geared toward a younger demographic. The Palms would have a fancy rooftop nightclub called Ghostbar. It would have a concert hall, the Pearl, which attracted major music acts crossing all genres. It had movie theaters, a big-time pool and spa, the requisite buffet and coffee shop as well as Garduno's, a popular Mexican restaurant which the Maloofs had started back in their native Albuquerque, New Mexico, after the family's Coors beer distributorship had taken off and become wildly successful.

As for the Kings, they had put a talented, young team on the floor that played exciting basketball. In 2002, the Kings made it to the NBA Western Conference Finals where they would challenge the Los Angeles Lakers. The Kings franchise, which dates back to the 1940s when they were the Rochester Royals, had won just one NBA title, in 1951. Now, they were on the precipice of getting back to the Finals.

However, the Lakers were talented and deep, and with Kobe Bryant and Shaquille O'Neal leading the way, along with a flurry of questionable calls in Game 6, the Lakers prevailed in seven games, clinching a spot in the Finals with a 112-106 overtime win.

That was as close as the Maloofs and the Kings would get to achieving greatness. The franchise began to struggle and with the team mired in Arco Arena, a building in the Sacramento suburbs that was quickly aging, the team tried to find a new home.

Contrast that to what was going on at the Palms, which had become the place to see and be seen. Things were going great in Las Vegas and Joe and Gavin Maloof wanted a similar scenario for their basketball team.

They engaged in a political battle to find a place to build a new arena in downtown Sacramento. But there was no appetite to spend public money on another sports facility. They enlisted the help of then-NBA commissioner David Stern, who believed in their market and did not want to see the Kings franchise move yet again. The team had relocated three times before, from Rochester to Cincinnati in 1957, then from Cincinnati to Kansas City in 1972, playing part of the home schedule in Omaha, Nebraska. In 1985, the third relocation took place as the Kings moved to Sacramento.

The Maloofs' frustration got to where they were considering leaving Sacramento. They looked at Anaheim, where the NHL's Ducks were established as the primary tenant. But the NBA already had the Lakers and the Clippers in that market. A third team might be too much.

Then in 2013, Chris Hansen, a Seattle billionaire who had made his fortune in hedge funds, met the Maloofs. The city had lost its NBA team, the SuperSonics, to Oklahoma City after Clay Bennett had purchased the team in 2008 and moved it.

Hansen wanted to bring the NBA back to Seattle. The negotiations picked up and the two sides had agreed to a deal.

However, Stern and the NBA were not ready to abandon Sacramento. The matter came to a vote in late April and the league's Board of Governors voted 22-8 not to approve the sale.

The Maloofs then entered into negotiations with Ranadive, another billionaire who made his money in computer software. He was a minority owner of the Golden State Warriors so he was familiar with the league. At the same time, another group of investors, led by Ron Burkle, was negotiating with the city of Sacramento to purchase a parcel of land downtown and convert stores located on the property into an arena for the Kings.

Burkle also had a sports background. He and Mario Lemieux had purchased the Pittsburgh Penguins, who were in danger of being moved to Kansas City in 2007. Not only did the Penguins, one of the NHL's Expansion Six teams from 1967 remain in Pittsburgh, but Burkle orchestrated the construction of a beautiful new arena. It opened in 2010 and became the home for the Penguins' two most recent Stanley Cup championships, in 2016 and 2017.

A deal was made with the city for a new arena for the Kings. The sale of the team to Ranadive was approved and the Maloofs were once again out of the sports business.

But they had $534 million on their hands, though the actual amount was less than half of that after paying off loans and other bills. Still, they had a lot of money and they were looking to get back into professional major league sports.

In the early fall of 2013, Joe and Gavin Maloof visited with Bettman. The commissioner knew the family from his days at the NBA when the Maloofs owned the Rockets. He liked them and when they inquired about getting into the NHL, Bettman listened.

The brothers saw that Las Vegas was growing. They thought it would be the ideal place for a hockey team. Bettman didn't disagree. In fact, as far back as 1999, Oscar Goodman, then the mayor of Las Vegas, had met with Bettman in the NHL's New York office and pitched the idea of hockey in the desert.

Bettman had several concerns, not the least of which was where a Las Vegas NHL team would play. There was truly no suitable facility in town for an NHL team. The Thomas & Mack Center, home to UNLV athletics, had tried hockey with the International Hockey League's Las Vegas Thunder. But the ice surface wasn't big enough for the NHL's requirements of 200 feet by 85 feet. The Thomas & Mack sheet was 10 feet short.

The MGM Grand Garden, which had a full-size NHL sheet, lacked capacity. It seated just over 11,000 for hockey and that wasn't even close to the NHL's minimum standard of 15,000.

Bettman also had concerns about the size of the market. There were just 1.3 million people living in all of Clark County at the time. From a television market size, Las Vegas was lagging behind, just 42nd on the list. For a league that was desperately trying to grow its brand, it didn't make sense to go into a small market, especially one with such little hockey history.

Then there was the issue of gambling. Sports betting was legal in Nevada, and Bettman wasn't comfortable at the time with having a franchise in a city where you could bet on the games, albeit legally.

Bettman told Goodman of his concerns, thanked him for his time and wished him luck.

Later that day, Goodman would meet with NBA commissioner David Stern who essentially told him no way would the league even consider putting a franchise in Las Vegas. Never mind that the Utah Jazz had played a dozen of its home games in 1984-85 at the Thomas & Mack. Stern was anti-gambling and no way was he going to acquiesce and put a team in a market where you could make a bet on the game.

Meanwhile, Las Vegas remained a special event city. World championship boxing matches continued to be held there. The emergence of Mixed Martial Arts found a home as the Fertitta family, which owned Station Casinos, made the city its home base for its Ultimate Fighting Championship.

Auto racing had a beautiful facility near Nellis Air Force Base at the Las Vegas Motor Speedway. NASCAR held an annual race there and other major motor sports events would stage races there.

Major League Baseball would have its teams come to town every spring for Big League Weekend at Cashman Field, drawing huge crowds. And while the NBA shunned the idea of putting a franchise in the city, the Los Angeles Lakers would make an annual visit to Las Vegas during the preseason. Eventually, so would their crosstown rivals, the Clippers.

Still, there was no major league professional sports team. There was a slew of football ventures, both indoors and outdoors. There were soccer teams which came and went along with a never-ending stream of basketball teams.

It appeared that was going to change in 2006.

There was talk of building a new arena. This one would be located on Koval Lane behind the Paris Las Vegas Hotel, which was owned by the company that owned Caesars Palace. The idea was build the arena and the NHL, and maybe even the NBA, would come. The NBA had agreed to hold its 2007 All-Star Game in Las Vegas, and Stern's stance on the city appeared to be softening.

A group of investors, including television and movie mogul Jerry Bruckheimer, were interested in an NHL franchise. The league, which had expanded to Columbus, Ohio, and St. Paul, Minnesota, six years before, wasn't ready to expand. But

Atlanta was struggling in its second venture with hockey and things in Phoenix weren't going so well with the Coyotes, who were having their own arena issues.

Maybe the timing was finally right for Las Vegas. There was hockey being played in the city as the Las Vegas Wranglers of the ECHL, the sport's Double-A league, was enjoying success playing at the 7,500-seat Orleans Arena. That facility had been built in 1996 by Michael Gaughan as part of the Orleans Hotel and Casino on West Tropicana Avenue, a couple of miles from the Strip.

The Los Angeles Kings were playing their own annual NHL preseason game, dubbed "Frozen Fury," at the MGM Grand Garden. The game was an annual sellout and it became a must-do event for Kings fans, both in Las Vegas and throughout Southern California.

The stars appeared to be in alignment.

Then came the Great Recession of 2008.

As America quickly spiraled economically, Las Vegas was hit particularly hard. Jobs disappeared. The value of homes cratered. Banks were not lending, instead trying to save themselves from shutting their own doors. It was the worst financial time the country had seen since the Great Depression following the stock market crash in 1929.

The planned arena behind the Paris was stopped and construction never began. Without a place to play, the NHL put Las Vegas on hold. And while the population had grown to 1.8 million, it wasn't enough to bring Las Vegas into the major leagues.

But the country and the community slowly recovered. And on May 1, 2014, MGM Grand officials announced they were partnering with the Anschutz Entertainment Group to construct a 20,000-seat arena behind the New York-New York and Monte Carlo hotels, just off the Las Vegas Strip.

The arena would be built with major league sports in mind, along with the requisite concerts, family shows and other events. AEG owned the Staples Center in Los Angeles and was also owner of the Los Angeles Kings, so it had a relationship with the NHL and Bettman.

The cost? $375 million. And it would have everything you would want in an arena — suites, roomy concourses, state-of-the-art scoreboards and sound systems, a plaza outside the arena where fans could congregate before games with bars and restaurants leading to the plaza.

This was exactly what the Maloofs had envisioned for the Sacramento Kings when they were the owners. A beautiful new arena, where tourists and locals could congregate and enjoy. And best of all, they wouldn't have to spend the money to build it themselves.

The timing couldn't be more perfect.

When the Maloofs met with Bettman about getting back into pro sports, little did they realize someone else had shared their vision and had beaten them to the punch.

Bill Foley was the founder and chairman of Fidelity National Financial Corporation, which provided insurance and claims management services. It was a publicly traded Fortune 500 company. He was based out of Jacksonville, Florida, not exactly a hotbed for hockey.

Foley had no interest in adding to Jacksonville's sports menu. The city had an NFL team, the Jaguars, and Foley had been approached to be a minority investor in the Jaguars.

"I wasn't really interested," Foley said.

But he was interested in hockey. And in Las Vegas.

Foley had been exposed to the sport as a kid while living in Ottawa. And while he was no expert, he was fascinated by the game and those who played it.

"I love everything about it," he said. "The people. The speed. The hitting. It's a great game."

Foley had attended the United States Military Academy at West Point, and after graduating in 1967 would go on to serve in the Air Force, attaining the rank of captain. His affection for the military would be evident later on.

Foley became a lawyer, specializing in real estate and corporate law. He set up a practice in Phoenix and it eventually led to an association with Fidelity. He eventually left practicing law to go into business, and he built Fidelity into one of the nation's largest insurance companies.

Foley also began to diversify, launching other businesses. He got into real estate. He opened restaurants. He invested in wine making.

Everything Foley touched seemed to be golden.

Athletically, Foley's passion was golf. Back in 2004, Golf Digest had rated him one of the "Top Five executive golfers in the world." He had developed a golf community in Montana and always tried to find time to play 18 holes whenever the opportunity presented itself.

It was suggested to Foley that he reach out to Bettman if he was serious about being an NHL owner. They had their first conversation in early 2014 and while Foley was prepared to foot the bill alone, be it for an expansion team, which was his preference, or buying an existing team and relocating it, Bettman suggested he look into taking on some limited partners.

Foley reached out to the Maloofs and a meeting was arranged in Florida. When the Maloofs got there, they were totally surprised.

"I couldn't believe that was Bill Foley," Gavin Maloof said. "I was expecting someone in a suit and tie, and here was a guy in a golf shirt and jeans. He was just like us."

If you've ever met Bill Foley, you would never guess he was a billionaire. Much like Warren Buffett, he is unassuming, low-key and enjoys talking to people. He is the kind of guy you could envision sitting with you at a bar over a beer or, in Foley's case, a glass of wine, and talking sports or politics for hours on end.

The two entities hit it off. "They're really good guys," Foley would say of the Maloofs.

They agreed they would pursue bringing the NHL to Las Vegas together. But the partnership had some parameters. One, Foley would be the main investor with the Maloofs serving as minority investors. Two, Foley, not the Maloofs, would be the public face of the venture and would speak for the group. Three, whatever decisions would be made would be Foley's and there would be no dissent.

"This has to be a dictatorship," Foley said half-kiddingly of the arrangement. "You can't have different people speaking. There has to be one voice."

The Maloofs agreed. They were used to being in the spotlight. Now, they were going to be out of sight, out of mind. It was a dramatic shift from their previous sports ventures. But they believed in Foley and they were certain that the NHL would be coming to Las Vegas, even though they had no assurances from Bettman that this would be the case. All they knew was they wanted back into major league sports and if it meant being in the shadows, so be it.

Meanwhile, groundbreaking on the MGM-AEG arena was taking place and construction quickly began after the May 1 ceremony which was attended by the Maloofs. Foley was not there. As summer turned to fall, the arena began to take shape. Unlike many cities, the weather in Las Vegas was conducive toward keeping construction projects either on or ahead of schedule.

The NHL was keeping its eye on things and in early December, Foley reached out to Bettman. He wanted the league's approval to launch a season ticket drive to gauge actual interest in the NHL by Las Vegas. The plan was to secure deposits from potential season ticket-holders with a minimum of $150 for a deposit per seat. The money would be kept in escrow and in the event the team failed to materialize, all investors would get their money back.

The goal was 10,000 deposits. Bettman thought that was a bit ambitious. After all, this wasn't Winnipeg where that city had lost the Jets to Phoenix in 1996 and was able to show it was ready to welcome back the NHL with 13,000 deposits in 2011 after the Atlanta Thrashers prepared to pull up stakes and move the franchise back to Manitoba's capital.

Yes, Las Vegas had hockey before. But this was the National Hockey League. The prices would be far steeper than those of the Thunder or the Wranglers. The commitment would also be greater.

For Foley, it was important to know whether he was wasting his time or if he had hit on the biggest and best idea of his life. The NHL was also receiving inquiries from the

Quebecor Corporation, which wanted to bring the NHL back to Quebec City after it had lost the Nordiques to Denver in 1996.

There was no doubt that Quebec would support hockey. Like Las Vegas, that city was building a state-of-the-art arena, the Videotron Centre, which would be a magnificent place to watch hockey.

The NHL had last expanded in 2000. Atlanta was the last relocation of a franchise and Bettman was't thrilled with the idea of teams packing up and moving. The Coyotes were not thriving in their new home in Glendale, Arizona, well off the beaten path from downtown Phoenix and the West Valley where the majority of their fan base resided.

In Florida, the Panthers were also struggling. The team had changed ownership and was trying to make things work in Sunrise, which was closer to the Everglades and alligators than it was to Miami Beach and its glitz and glamour.

The easy thing would be to just move the Coyotes to Las Vegas and the Panthers to Quebec. But Bettman had other ideas.

When the Columbus Blue Jackets and Minnesota Wild joined the NHL in 2000, the expansion fee was $80 million apiece. What if the NHL expanded again, this time to 32 teams, and charged Foley and Quebecor far more to join?

Bettman and Foley talked and the league gave Foley the green light to run his season ticket drive. On Feb. 10, 2015, at the MGM Grand, with Bettman in attendance and hockey players skating on plastic ice, Foley announced "Vegas Wants Hockey" and a goal to procure 10,000 deposits by the end of June.

At the end of the first day, the drive was already halfway to its goal as more than 5,000 deposits had been placed online. Foley was stunned.

"I was hoping we'd get 2,500 sold that first day," Foley said. "I honestly didn't know what to expect. But it was amazing to have several hundred businessmen, several politicians, having the commissioner on the stage. I thought it was impressive."

Two weeks later, the number grew to 6,500. By the end of March, they had reached their goal. By June, more than 14,000 had put down money for a team which did not exist, had no name, no colors, no logo, no players, no coach, no general manager.

It was the ultimate leap of faith. In concert with the drive, Foley had formed a group of local businessmen, civic leaders and celebrities to help push tickets. The "Founding 50" as they were known were charged with selling 60 season tickets each.

The Founding 50 quickly grew to 60, then 75. And while their purpose was noble, it wasn't needed when it came to peddling tickets. The community had seen to that with its response.

But it would be a sure sign that the city's power brokers were on board with the attempt to bring a major league sports team to Las Vegas.

At the time, there was only a couple of employees at what was known as Black Knight Sports and Entertainment, the company Foley had formed to launch his hockey venture. Todd Pollock, who was charged with overseeing the ticket drive, had been hired the month before the launch. He had worked in sports before, both in college and in the pros. He had been employed by the Los Angeles Kings for three years so he knew something about hockey and selling the game.

But this was bigger than anything he had experienced. He was going to have to sort through more than 14,000 requests, figure out the fairest way to prioritize who sat where and learn to say "No."

But it was a nice problem to have. And with the drive a resounding success, the next step was to join the NHL.

2. Dreams To Reality

At the 2015 Stanley Cup Finals, the talk of expansion was heating up. Bettman acknowledged that the NHL was considering expansion for the first time since 2000 but would not say how many teams or which cities.

Foley knew better. Las Vegas was very much on the NHL's radar and Foley was starting to put together a staff in the event the league granted him a franchise.

Costs were speculating on how much it would be. Some said $200 million. Others thought $300 million or $350 million, any of which would have been a record amount to join the NHL.

The league's Board of Governors had an expansion committee which delved into the possibilities and would report back to the entire membership. The committee would do its due diligence on the viability of the groups that were interested, primarily Black Knight Sports and entertainment and Quebecor Corporation. Both would submit to background checks as to their financial health.

Back in the mid-1990s, the NHL got burned when John Spano bought the New York Islanders based on a bankroll of deceit and fraud. The NHL was embarrassed when news came out that Spano had virtually no means to own a hockey team and he had swindled banks and other lending institutions to keep him financially liquid.

The NHL was determined that would never happen again. So Foley turned in reams of paperwork and submitted to numerous questions. An FBI background check was a piece of cake compared to what the NHL was putting him through.

But Foley understood it was part of doing business. And when the deadline to apply for a franchise came and went on July 20, 2015, Foley had sent the NHL ten million dollars. So had Quebec City. They would be the lone applicants.

As the due diligence process continued, Foley learned the meaning of patience.

"I'm not a very patient person by nature," he said. "But I know I'm going to have to learn to be as we go through this process."

The Board of Governors met in Pebble Beach, California, in December and there was speculation a decision might be at hand. But Bettman said at the meeting that no decision had been reached and the process would continue into 2016. He wouldn't comment on whether there were any issues with Foley's application but those in the know said Foley's role was no problem.

The league was more concerned about the arena and the legal gambling issue, more concerns about the former than the latter. The arena was progressing nicely and was looking at an April 2016 opening. Officials were finalizing a deal in which telephone provider T-Mobile would obtain the naming rights for the building, which would seat approximately 17,500 for hockey.

As for gambling, the NHL, like the other pro sports leagues, had a relationship with the Las Vegas sports books.

The books maintained a dialogue with the leagues and would keep them apprised of any suspicious betting activity.

Hockey had no betting scandals to speak of and the reality was that the NHL generated very little handle — less than five percent — in the overall amount of bets the books took in. The danger of tainting the game was minuscule at best.

As the 2016 season headed to the playoffs, the rumors began to heat up. Word was Las Vegas was in but the owners were not quite sure about Quebec City. There were reportedly concerns over the strength of the Canadian dollar and whether it was strong enough to make a Quebec NHL franchise profitable. The loonie had sunk to 68 cents compared to the American dollar, and with that kind of instability, the owners were worried that Quebec City would make it.

At the Stanley Cup Final in Pittsburgh, Bettman said no final decision had been reached. But on June 15, word was the Board of Governors executive committee had recommended the league expand to Las Vegas only.

That would leave the NHL with an odd number of teams — 31. It also meant the balance of the conferences would remain uneven, 16 in the East, 15 in the West. That imbalance also was a cause for concern about putting a team in Quebec. It couldn't realistically put Quebec in the West and if Quebec were put in the East where it belonged, it would have meant convincing another Eastern Conference owner (Detroit? Columbus?) to move their franchise to the West. And that would have been a tough sell.

The NHL had been holding its Awards Show in Las Vegas since 2007. So with everyone in town to see who picked up the various trophies and honors, it made sense for the league to hold its Board of Governors meeting in town.

On the morning of June 22, 2016, the owners met at the Encore Hotel to make the decision. The asking price to join? A record $500 million. Foley, who pretty much knew what the verdict would be, stayed coy and optimistic.

"We have done everything we were asked to," he said.

Before a packed ballroom, Bettman announced what Las Vegas fans had eagerly anticipated and Quebec fans had been dreading — the NHL was expanding to 31 teams and Las Vegas would be the 31st.

"Well, Las Vegas, we did it!" Foley said. "We want everyone to be a fan and we're dedicated to it. My obligation is to hold the trust of this team for the community."

And as Las Vegas celebrated the news, those in Quebec were left with an empty feeling. Rejection is always difficult and to be passed over for a city that had very little hockey history hurt deeply. The Quebecor group said all the right things. But the words rang hollow.

That evening a celebration was held at the team's temporary offices in the Donald Reynolds Foundation building adjacent to the TPC Summerlin golf course. In the courtyard with hundreds of invited guests holding flutes of champagne, Clark County commissioner Steve Sisolak offered a toast to Foley and his NHL expansion team, one that still did not have a name, a logo, colors, players, a coach or a general manager.

But that was about to change quickly.

Bill Foley had his franchise. Now he had to build a team.

There would be no shortage of attractive candidates when it came to filling the general manager's chair. There were plenty of smart, experienced hockey executives who would jump at the chance to build a team from scratch.

As the 2016 calendar quickly flipped from June to July, Foley knew he had to move quickly. He was going to need people to scout and assess the 30 NHL teams in preparation for the expansion draft scheduled for the following June. He also would need scouts to watch amateur hockey as well as the professional leagues in Europe.

Those hirings could not be made until he had a general manager. But who would be the right person? Foley wanted someone he felt comfortable with, someone he could trust to make the right decisions while spending his money wisely.

This would be arguably the biggest decision he would make and he couldn't afford to get it wrong. This couldn't just be a gut call where you think you have a feeling it will work out in the end. And unlike real estate or insurance or wine, Foley wasn't well versed in the business of hockey. Sure, he knew what the salary cap was. He was aware of analytics even though he couldn't tell you what Corsi was. He was not aware of all the rules regarding free agency, trades, draft picks and things like that.

And while Foley was making every attempt to gain knowledge of such matters, the reality was he was hardly going to qualify as an expert. So he had to hire someone who was.

But who would that someone be? Would it be someone who was already a general manager, someone who had built a team from the start, such as Nashville's David Poile? Would it be a GM who had experience, someone like Florida's Dale Tallon or Don Waddell in Carolina? Would he go for an assistant general manager who had paid his dues and was ready to move up, someone like Norm Maciver in Chicago, Paul Fenton in Nashville or Jason Botterill in Pittsburgh?

Foley picked the brains of his fellow owners. He also did his own homework. And when he began the process in early July at his ranch in Montana, far away from the prying eyes of the Las Vegas media, Foley quickly found his man.

George McPhee had built the Washington Capitals into one of the NHL's elite franchises. In his first season, 1998, the Capitals made it to the Stanley Cup Final, only to be swept by the Detroit Red Wings. McPhee always had a reputation for being smart, for having a keen eye for assessing talent, for hiring good people and allowing them to do their jobs and knowing how to work within the framework of the NHL rule book. He also understood the league's salary cap and hired people who really knew it. He had scouts all over the world looking for the next great star player.

In other words, George McPhee was exactly what Bill Foley was looking for. What's more, McPhee was highly motivated? Capitals owner Ted Leonsis opted not to renew McPhee's contract following the 2014-15 season, after the Caps flopped in the playoffs. McPhee had spent 17 years in the nation's capital and the fact he wouldn't be allowed to see his handiwork through to the end had to sting.

He was able to stay in the game thanks to Hockey Canada, which made him an assistant general manager for the 2016 World Championships, and the New York Islanders hired him as a special assistant to general manager Garth Snow.

But the big question was, would McPhee and Foley hit it off?

It didn't take Foley long to realize he had his man after sitting down with McPhee for the first time.

"We were on the same page," Foley said. "I felt George was someone I could trust to do the right thing and build our hockey club the right way."

On July 12, 2017, in a small conference room at T-Mobile Arena, McPhee was announced as the general manager of the Las Vegas NHL franchise. The team still didn't have a name or a logo, but Foley was working on that. The important thing was he had his general manager in place.

"I have complete faith in George," Foley said. "I knew right away after talking to him for the first time that he was the one I wanted to lead our franchise.

"I was looking for a guy who was going to be as focused, dedicated, have a take-no-prisoners attitude and who was as committed to winning. But more important, someone I could identify with, have a symbiotic relationship with, and that we could have a respectful relationship where we can talk freely and honestly. I found that person, and I'm really thrilled."

McPhee was equally thrilled to be back in the big chair, saying, "Every general manager dreams of having this kind of opportunity, to build a team from the very beginning. I'm grateful and excited to be here, and we will put a product on the ice that Las Vegas can be proud of and win a Stanley Cup."

Little did he know that day how prophetic his words would ultimately be.

McPhee had been a scrappy player. He was a star at Bowling Green University and in 1982, he won the Hobey Baker Award, which goes to college hockey's best player. He would play seven NHL seasons with the New York Rangers and New Jersey Devils, and he scored 21 goals and had 24 assists in 109 games. He also racked up 247 penalty minutes and at 5 feet, 9 inches and just 170 pounds, McPhee had to show he would not back down from the game's bigger, rougher and tougher players.

After his playing career ended, he got his law degree and became a player agent. Eventually, he got into hockey management as an assistant to Vancouver Canucks General Manager Pat Quinn. During his time in Vancouver, the Canucks made four playoff appearances and reached the Stanley Cup Final in 1994, only to lose to McPhee's old team, the Rangers, in Game 7. The Rangers had ended a decades-long hex with their first championship since 1940.

McPhee moved on to Washington in 1997 as the Capitals' general manager and he made hockey relevant in the nation's capital. And while the Caps struggled for a bit after reaching the final in '98, McPhee drafted wisely and quickly rebuilt the team to where the Capitals were among the best in the league.

He drafted Alex Ovechkin, Nicklas Backstrom, John Carlson, Evgeny Kuznetsov and Braden Holtby, the core of the Caps' 2018 Stanley Cup championship team.

Now, he was starting anew. His first order of business in Las Vegas was to hire an assistant and build a hockey staff. For McPhee, one name jumped out.

Kelly McCrimmon had been a vanguard in junior hockey, one of the most respected individuals at that level of the game. McCrimmon had built a strong program with the Brandon Wheat Kings, having served as the team's coach, general manager and eventually, the owner. The Wheaties, as they're known in their hometown, had made three Memorial Cup appearances while McCrimmon was the team's GM and he was a hot commodity for NHL teams looking for a junior executive.

The Toronto Maple Leafs had pursued McCrimmon but he elected to stay in Brandon, which is about a two-hour drive from Winnipeg.

However, when McPhee called about coming to Las Vegas, McCrimmon was interested. He would have a bigger role with the expansion team, and he knew his advice would be critical when it came time to select players in both the NHL expansion draft and the league's amateur draft come 2017.

Foley met McCrimmon, and as with McPhee, they hit it off. It didn't hurt that Murray Craven, who at the time was serving as an adviser to Foley on all matters in hockey, had known McCrimmon and knew of his acumen.

As July was ending, McPhee was moving quickly. Almost daily there was news of another hire. Vaughn Karpan was brought in as the team's director of player personnel. Bob Lowes was brought on to be the assistant director of player personnel. Scott Luce was hired as the team's director of amateur scouting. David Conte was named special advisor for hockey operations. Wil Nichol was tabbed to be the team's director of player development. Misha Donskov was to oversee hockey operations.

Craven, who was already working on plans for the team's practice facility, was named senior vice president. Andrew Lugerner, who worked for McPhee in Washington, was brought on to handle salary cap questions as the team's director of legal affairs. Tom Poraszka, who had built a successful online venture for salary cap nerds with GeneralFanger.com, was lured away to assist with cap issues.

McPhee also convinced Katy Boettinger, who was his right-hand person at the office in Washington, to leave a teaching job in Florida to return to pro sports as the director of hockey administration in Las Vegas.

Just as quickly, scouts were being hired, both pro and amateur. Erin Ginnell, Bruno Campese, Raphael Pouliot, Peter Ward, Kent Hawley, Mark Workman and Mike Levine all began work as members of the team's amateur scouting staff. On the pro side, Vince Williams, Kelly Kisio, Jim McKenzie, Alex Godynyuk, Peter Ahola, Mike Rosati and Vaclav Nedomansky were brought in to scout in the NHL as well as Europe.

The first amateur tournament, the Ivan Hlinka Memorial Cup, was getting ready to start in mid-August in Bratislava, and Las Vegas would be well represented.

In addition, the training camps for junior teams, college teams and, of course, the NHL, were just weeks away. And for the next 10 months, McPhee and his hockey people would be all over the world watching, evaluating and taking copious notes in preparation for the two drafts that would come 48 hours apart in June 2017.

It was truly an exciting time. For McPhee, this is what he lived for.

"We built some terrific teams in Washington. Then they took the canvas and the paint brushes away," he said. "Now they're giving me something which is brand new, and I get the chance to start fresh."

3. Building A Franchise

The 2016-17 NHL season was underway. T-Mobile Arena had already hosted its first hockey games as the Los Angeles Kings had played the Dallas Stars and the Colorado Avalanche during the preseason in the first weekend of October.

The arena had drawn rave reviews from fans who loved the sightlines, the easy access in and out of the building, the proximity to the Las Vegas Strip and the variety of beverage options. It seemed you only had to walk a couple of feet anywhere in the arena and come face to face with a beer, or something stronger.

Bill Foley didn't mind the Kings having a trial run in his team's arena. Any bugs that needed to be worked out could be addressed, whether it was the quality of the ice, the locker rooms, the ticketing procedure, parking or any other issue that came up.

Now, as Thanksgiving was approaching, this remained a team without a name, a logo or colors. Fans were antsy. What was their team going to be called? When could they get a jersey?

There had been contests in the media to solicit names for the team. It ran the gamut from gambling monikers (Aces, Blackjacks, Gamblers) to Outlaws, Wranglers and Strip-pers.

But in his mind, Foley had only one name — Black Knights. After all, he was a West Point graduate. Black Knights was a noble name. It was also the name of Army's athletic teams. Certainly, those in charge at West Point wouldn't mind.

Would they?

It turns out the name met with some resistance. But Foley was determined to find a way to incorporate "Knights" into his team's name. Working with the NHL's legal department and creative services, Foley was leaning toward "Golden Knights." But there were potential legal ramifications with that name. For starters, the Army's parachute team was named the Golden Knights. And at the Pentagon, they didn't take kindly to someone using that name.

In addition, a number of colleges, big and small, had Golden Knights as their nickname for their sports teams. In some cases, such as Clarkson and Central Florida, Foley and Peter Sadowski, the team's legal affairs person, got the schools' blessing. But the College of Saint Rose, a school in Albany, New York, also had the Golden Knights moniker and they weren't happy about a hockey team using it.

Still, the team filed trademark applications for the name "Vegas Golden Knights". And on November 22, with 5,000 fans crowded in what was now known as Toshiba Plaza outside T-Mobile Arena and with Bettman in attendance, the name "Vegas Golden Knights" was announced.

The team's colors would be steel gray, black, gold and red. The logo, a gold medieval knight's helmet with a black "V" embedded in it, was placed within a pentagon-sided crest.

There was a glitch with the video to announce the name and logo, and that didn't sit well with Foley. But what could he do? In professional sports, things don't always go according to plan.

The response on social media was swift. Some loved the name. Others hated it. Some wanted to know why not "Las Vegas" instead of just "Vegas"? The logo seemed OK to the majority. The gray, black and gold color scheme didn't seem that offensive.

Long lines formed to get the first T-shirts and hats. Unfortunately, the jerseys would not be available for another nine months. The NHL had changed sportswear partners, and adidas, which was taking over for Reebok as the league's official jersey manufacturer, was not set up to produce a Golden Knights jersey in November.

Meanwhile, the Department of the Army challenged the hockey team's Golden Knights trademark and it would take more than a year for the matter to be resolved as attorneys for both sides worked on an agreement the two parties could live with.

Foley had his hockey people hard at work. Now, he was in need of building the business side of his team's operation. Just a couple of weeks before the announcement of the team's name and logo, Foley hired Kerry Bubolz to serve as team president. Bubolz had worked for the Cleveland Cavaliers as the NBA team's president of business operations. He also had worked in sales for the Dallas Stars and Carolina Hurricanes, so he had hockey experience. In addition, Bubolz had served as president of the American Hockey League's Cleveland Lumberjacks from 1994 to 2000.

At the same time, ground was broken for the team's practice facility. After looking at a couple of different locations, Foley settled on a parcel of land owned by the Howard Hughes

Corporation. It was located directly across from the Downtown Summerlin Shopping Center. With the 215 Beltway nearby, providing easy access to McCarran International Airport, and just 20 to 25 minutes from T-Mobile Arena, it was an ideal location. Besides, there was affordable housing nearby and the majority of the players figured to live near where they would work out and practice, which made the location even more appealing.

The plans called for two sheets of ice, a main locker room, a player's lounge, coaches' offices, meeting rooms, sports medicine facilities, weight and strength areas and nine locker rooms for youth and adult hockey, which would be a big part of the facility.

In addition, there would be a restaurant and bar on the second floor and stands to accommodate 600 fans in each rink. The team's offices would also relocate from the Reynolds Foundation building in Summerlin to the practice facility.

By now, more than 100 employees had been hired in various departments, including marketing, promotions, media relations, business ticketing and suites and entertainment. The new offices would put everyone under one roof.

There would also be a team store that would be fully stocked and would also serve as a pro shop where players could buy equipment if needed and get their skates sharpened without having to travel elsewhere in town.

The challenge? Have the facility ready for training camp come September 2017. Murray Craven, who had been in plenty of rinks in his hockey career, was charged with the project. He would put in long days over the next 10 months as the building took form.

The hockey gods apparently were with Craven. There were no mishaps and construction, which was handled by a local outfit, Gillett Construction, went off with nary a hitch.

Ten months and close to $31 million later, City National Arena, as the facility was branded, opened its doors in August, in plenty of time for training camp. Foley initially thought the cost would be half as much. But with the cost of land and materials rising, so did the price tag. In the end, he wasn't complaining.

For the community, it would be a place to gather. It would serve as a home for the Junior Golden Knights youth hockey program, as the team joined forces with the Nevada Storm youth program and used the NHL team's brand to attract new players.

For Bubolz, identifying and growing the next generation of fans was critical to the team's long-term success. And youth hockey was going to be a huge component. But how do you get kids interested?

Late in the spring of 2017, the team began a "Sticks For Kids" program where clinics were held at community recreation centers around Las Vegas. The team also participated in the NHL's "Learn to play for Free" program where boys and girls ages 5 to 9 would be fully outfitted and taught the basic skills of the sport at no cost.

According to statistics from USA Hockey, Nevada was fourth from the bottom in terms of participants prior to the Golden Knights' arrival, with just 1,342 players. In 2017, there were more than 1,600 registered youth players in the Silver State. USA Hockey oversees the sport and is responsible for helping grow the game.

The facility also served as a home for youth and adult hockey tournaments and it had to be a thrill for a kid from Texas to skate on the same ice an NHL team practices on. For the players in the Junior Golden Knights program, it was a chance to play the game at a higher level, traveling around North America to compete in tournaments and being able to improve without leaving home.

In January, the team announced it was partnering with the Clark County School District to have hockey become part of the physical education curriculum at the middle school level. It was a huge step toward exposing the game to kids and those youth hockey numbers figure to grow in the years ahead.

Now that the team had a name and an identity, it still needed players and someone to coach them.

The NHL's general manager meetings are held annually in early March, usually in Boca Raton, Florida. But George McPhee wasn't officially invited. At least not yet.

Before McPhee could officially attend any meetings, his owner had to pay up. For Bill Foley, that meant sending the remainder of the $500 million he had paid for the Golden Knights franchise. Foley had made two earlier payments and with the date of the GM meetings drawing close, he didn't want to hamstring his guy.

A couple of days before the meetings, the league received the remainder of the $500 million. McPhee was now welcome to attend. He "celebrated" by taking a swim in the Atlantic Ocean.

It was an important meeting and McPhee definitely needed to be there. The NHL's rules for the expansion draft had been formulated, and deputy commissioner Bill Daly was in Florida to help answer any questions. McPhee had already been made aware of what the basic rules would be for the expansion draft, which would be held June 22 at T-Mobile Arena and televised nationally on the NBC Sports Network.

This was a huge event for the NHL and it wanted to make sure everyone was on the same page when it came to understanding the parameters surrounding the expansion draft.

McPhee and Daly would hold a number of conversations before the draft. Mostly for clarification on certain rules.

Meanwhile, college free agency was at hand. Any player who had not been drafted was eligible to sign with an NHL team. Same for a junior player who had never been drafted and was 20 years of age or older.

On March 6, the team announced its first-ever player signing. Reid Duke, a center who played for Kelly McCrimmon's Brandon Wheat Kings, became the answer to a trivia question. Duke, a 6-foot, 191-pounder from Calgary had spent six years in junior hockey, first with Lethbridge, then with Brandon. He had played in the shadow of Nolan Patrick, the Wheat Kings' star player who many were projecting to be there No. 1 overall pick in the 2017 draft.

But Patrick was dealing with a sports hernia injury which kept him sidelined for a good portion of the season and it gave Duke a chance to play a more dominant role. He had a career-high 37 goals and 34 assists for 71 points.

The Knights had their first player. But they still didn't have a coach. McPhee actually knew who he wanted and it appeared he was going to get his man. It was just a matter of being patient and hoping some other team didn't get to him first.

In 2015-16, Gerard Gallant had led the Florida Panthers to the Atlantic Division title and a spot in the playoffs. He was a finalist for the Jack Adams Award, which goes to the NHL's Coach of the Year. His players loved playing for him and he had an easy-going way about him.

He also was very competitive. As a player, he skated with Steve Yzerman as teammates with the Detroit Red Wings, and Gallant was a tough guy who also had some skills and could put the puck into the net. He played 11 seasons in the NHL, scored 211 goals and racked up 1,674 penalty minutes.

After he retired, Gallant got into coaching. He was an assistant in the minor leagues for two years, then joined the Columbus Blue Jackets as an assistant. In 2004 he was promoted to interim head coach of the Blue Jackets and spent parts of three seasons in that capacity. After the Blue Jackets let him go, Gallant spent two years with the New York Islanders as an assistant before going back to junior hockey to serve as head coach at Saint John of the Quebec Major Junior Hockey League. He won two league titles along with the Memorial Cup in 2011.

It was there that his reputation as a players' coach was fostered. He wanted his players to have fun when they came to the rink and work hard during the time they were there.

The Montreal Canadiens took notice and they hired Gallant as an assistant in 2012. Two years later, he was once again an NHL head coach, this time with the Florida Panthers. The Panthers were in the process of a rebuild and they had some talented young players. Dale Tallon, the team's general manager at the time, wanted someone who could relate to the youngsters, motivate them and help them grow.

In his first season in 2015, Gallant guided the Panthers to 38 wins. It might have been more but Florida had 15 overtime or shootout losses. But the following year, the Panthers won 47 games, captured the Atlantic Division with 103 points and made the playoffs. But Florida lost a hard-fought opening-round series to the Islanders.

Still, the future looked bright in Sunrise, Florida. That was until management decided to make some drastic changes. Tallon, who had drafted wisely and traded to build a competitive team, was kicked upstairs. Tom Rowe was now the general manager. Ownership was convinced that analytics was the way to build a winner and the team's entire philosophy took a 180-degree turn.

Gallant, as old-school a hockey guy as you'll get, tried to continue coaching his team his way. But with the Panthers off to a slow start in 2016-17 and some key players being injured, management's patience began to shrink. And on November 27, after losing 3-2 to the Carolina Hurricanes, Gallant was fired.

His belongings and those of assistant coach Mike Kelly were taken off the team bus. The Panthers had sent for a car to take the two former coaches to the Raleigh, North Carolina Airport. But when the ride never showed up, Gallant called for a taxi.

The now-famous picture of Gallant and Kelly getting in the cab spoke to the bizarre nature of how things were handled and the gaffe Florida management had committed.

Gallant was understandably upset and confused. He knew coaching in the NHL was a results-driven business. But hadn't he delivered? Was it his fault he didn't have a full compliment of players? He didn't ask the team to change its philosophy.

A couple of weeks passed and Gallant was starting to get on with his life. Then his phone rang. It was George McPhee. The Golden Knights' general manager was looking for a head coach for his expansion hockey team and would Gallant be interested in sitting down and talking to him?

Gallant was absolutely interested. He and McPhee met, and McPhee knew right away he had his guy. Yes, he would look at other candidates. But if Bill Foley was comfortable with Gallant, and Gallant was willing to wait until after the regular season, he would likely be the choice.

Foley and Gallant hit it off. Gallant did have some suitors, namely the Islanders, who were letting Jack Capuano go. But Gallant seemed comfortable with Vegas and on April 13, 2017, Gallant was at T-Mobile Arena being introduced as the first head coach of the Vegas Golden Knights.

"I knew it was the right fit for me," Gallant said. "In talking to George and Bill Foley, I saw the direction they wanted to go, and having had experience with an expansion team when I was with Columbus as an assistant, I knew this was a great opportunity."

McPhee said: "We had time on our side, and when you have it, you use it. We didn't have players to coach. There were so many other things we needed to do before we hired a coach, and in going through the process, there were some people who requested we wait until the end of the season to contact."

In taking the job, Gallant was assured that McPhee would not meddle, that he would be allowed to coach the team as he saw fit. Who played and who didn't would be his decision.

He quickly brought Mike Kelly into the fold as his associate head coach. The two had worked well together in Florida and Gallant knew he could trust Kelly. He also hired Ryan McGill, who had been the head coach of the Owen Sound Attack in the Ontario Hockey League, and he brought in Ryan Craig, who had just wrapped up his playing career and had no coaching experience. But Craig was young, just 35, and he would likely relate well to the young players who would be wearing the Knights' sweater come fall.

The one coach Gallant didn't have a hand in hiring was David Prior, the team's goaltender coach. McPhee hired Prior early in his tenure. The two had worked together in Washington and Prior, whose methods for teaching the position aren't traditional, was someone who got results.

Gallant wasn't worried. "I don't know anything about goaltending," he said.

Meanwhile, McPhee and his hockey operations staff were shifting into high gear. The expansion draft and entry draft were less than two months away. They were running out of time to prepare.

4. The Knights Take Shape

The team that finally had a name, a logo, colors and a coach was preparing to take the biggest step yet, filling out a roster.

The Golden Knights were to take part in the NHL Draft Lottery on April 29 in Chicago. The hope was they would get one of the top two picks and likely choose either Nolan Patrick of the Brandon Wheat Kings or Nico Hischier of the Halifax Mooseheads.

The lottery is weighted and each team is assigned a percentage of probability in winning the top pick. Thus the Knights had a 10.3 percent chance of getting the No. 1 pick.

A watch party was held at T-Mobile Arena and one of the guests was a good luck charm nicknamed "Stanley". Stanley was a ceramic rooster who had been gifted to Bill Foley by the executives of the Oriental Mandarin Hotel during the Chinese New Year celebration in February. It was supposed to bring the team good luck.

Stanley took its rightful place near one of the televisions and the process began. And when NHL deputy commissioner Bill Daly announced that the Knights would have the No. 6 pick, a collective groan was let out. New Jersey would pick first, followed by Philadelphia and Dallas.

So much for luck. But as it would turn out, Stanley would redeem itself a year later.

Adding to the bad karma that day was general manager George McPhee, who was supposed to be in Toronto for the lottery, was stuck in Washington due to bad weather and never made it.

Still, the Knights figured to get a good player at No. 6. But that was a ways off. They were still looking for free agents to sign and join Reid Duke and they thought they had landed a big one when they announced the signing of Vadim Shipachyov, a 30-year-old center from Russia who had been playing in the Continental Hockey League. The deal was for two years, $9 million, and the belief was "Shippy," as he was called, would be a top-six forward, maybe even center the team's first line.

On June 1, the Knights signed free-agent forward Tomas Hyka, who had been initially drafted by Los Angeles in 2012 and had yet to play in the NHL. So the roster was now at three players.

The big day was looming, however.

The NHL Expansion Draft was scheduled for June 21 at T-Mobile Arena. The Knights would select one player from each of the existing 30 NHL teams to fill out their roster. Teams had the option to protect one goaltender, three defensemen and seven forwards, or one goalie and eight skaters, a mix of forwards and defensemen. Teams would also be allowed to make side deals with Vegas to protect players who were eligible to be selected.

McPhee would have to select a minimum of three goaltenders, nine defensemen and 14 forwards. The remaining four players were his choice.

As the expansion draft drew near, there was much speculation as to what the Knights would do. Would they take five or six goalies? Would they go for youth over experience? Would they be willing to take on a bad contract in order to acquire additional assets (i.e., draft picks)?

McPhee, who would make a great poker player, never tipped his hand. And as he and Foley walked to the stage for what was tantamount to a game show, McPhee felt confident.

"I knew we had done our homework," he said. "We were prepared and out staff did a tremendous job of scouting and evaluating."

The team had also gone through several mock draft exercises going back to October. They would spend two or three days going through every scenario. And when they had a question concerning a rule, they called Daly for an answer.

With the event being televised throughout North America, and more than 14,000 fans inside T-Mobile Arena, the process began. Calvin Pickard, a goaltender from the Colorado Avalanche, would be the first player taken in the expansion draft.

Here's how the entire draft went:

From Anaheim: Defenseman Clayton Stoner. In addition, the Knights got defenseman Shea Theodore for having selected Stoner.

From Arizona: Forward Teemu Pulkkinen.

From Boston: Defenseman Colin Miller.

From Buffalo: Forward Will Carrier. In addition, the Knights received a sixth-round draft pick.

From Calgary: Defenseman Deryk Engelland.

From Carolina: Forward Connor Brickley. In addition, the Knights received a fifth-round draft pick.

From Chicago: Defenseman Trevor van Riemsdyk.

From Colorado: Pickard.

From Columbus: Forward William Karlsson. In addition, the Knights received a 2017 first-round draft pick, a 2019 second-round draft pick and the contract of forward David Clarkson.

From Dallas: Center Cody Eakin.

From Detroit: Forward Tomas Nosek.

From Edmonton: Defenseman Griffin Reinhart.

From Florida: Forward Jonathan Marchessault. In addition, the Knights acquired forward Reilly Smith for a 2018 fourth-round draft pick.

From Los Angeles: Defenseman Brayden McNabb.

From Minnesota: Center Erik Haula. The Knights also acquired forward Alex Tuch for a third-round draft pick.

From Montreal: Defenseman Alexi Emelin.

From Nashville: Forward James Neal.

From New Jersey: Defenseman Jon Merrill.

From New York Islanders: Goaltender Jean-Francois Berube. The Knights also acquired forward Mikhail Grabovski, defenseman Jake Bischoff, a 2017 first-round draft pick, and a 2019 second-round draft pick.

From New York Rangers: Forward Oscar Lindberg.

From Ottawa: Defenseman Marc Methot.

From Philadelphia: Center Pierre-Edouard Bellemare.

From Pittsburgh: Goaltender Marc-Andre Fleury. The Knights also received a second-round draft pick in 2020.

From San Jose: Defenseman David Schlemko.

From St. Louis: Forward David Perron.

From Tampa Bay: Defenseman Jason Garrison. The Knights also acquired the NHL rights to forward Nikita Gusev, a 2017 second-round draft pick, and a 2018 fourth-round pick.

From Toronto: Forward Brendan Leipsic.

From Vancouver: Defenseman Luca Sbisa.

From Washington: Defenseman Nate Schmidt.

From Winnipeg: Forward Chris Thorburn. The Knights also traded the Columbus first-round pick (No. 24 overall) for the No. 13 overall pick and a third-round draft pick.

Fleury, whose name was among the last called, received the loudest cheers. His was easily the most recognizable face, and the fans who were in the arena and watched on television could not help but think that their team had at least one big-time player to build around.

Fleury, who was on hand when his name was called, was just as thrilled.

"I'm excited to be with a new team and a new organization," he said. "By the way the crowd was tonight and the way the team is looking, I am excited."

"I'm not looking to be the face of much — I just want to come in and play hockey. I will give everything I've got to win some games as well as getting into the community to meet people and spread the word about the Vegas Golden Knights."

His new teammates were also looking forward to a fresh start.

"I was surprised also, but it is part of the game and if you look at all the guys Florida protected, they're all great hockey players," Marchessault said. "It was a hard decision I'm sure for them, but it is part of the game. You can't take it personally, it's a business. Everybody was asking me if I was going to be protected or not and my answer was I gave everything I had and after that, I had no regrets. I'm just happy with my season. I want to go there and improve every year. I just want to help my team win every night. Now it is up to me to respond."

Engelland, who had met his wife Melissa when he played for the Las Vegas Wranglers, was also excited.

"I started here as a Wrangler," Engelland said. "To be here and put this jersey on is an honor."

McPhee said he had two objectives in mind when it came to the expansion draft. "One was to put an entertaining team on the ice that the NHL and Las Vegas can be proud of," he said. "The second was to acquire prospects and draft picks that can help us build our team in the future."

But McPhee's work was far from finished. The NHL Entry Draft was a couple of days away in Chicago and he, McCrimmon and the rest of the hockey operations staff were on a plane to the Windy City shortly after the expansion draft had wrapped up.

Thanks to his deals with Columbus and the Islanders, McPhee found himself with three picks in the first 15 selections. He thought about packaging the picks in an attempt to move up to the top spot, but in the end, he stayed with what he had.

The Knights would pick sixth, 13th and 15th. And while the expansion draft yielded a varied group of players, McPhee was looking for a couple of things in particular in the entry draft.

The first was speed. He knew the NHL game was quicker and it didn't matter what position you played, you just better be able to skate fast.

The second was smarts. McPhee was a smart hockey player when he played and he has always valued intelligence in a player. Nicklas Backstrom, who has one of the highest hockey IQs in the league, was a first-round pick by McPhee when he was the general manager in Washington. So whoever he took better be able to think the game when he was on the ice.

The draft, which was kicked off with the always-stirring rendition of the Star-Spangled Banner by legendary anthem singer Jim Cornelison, got the United Center crowd in the right mood. Every team's fan base was represented, including some Golden Knights fans who had made the trip from Las Vegas.

The question was, who would go first? Nolan or Nico? The Devils provided the answer by selecting Hischier, who was from Switzerland and had a big season with Halifax.

The Flyers took Patrick with the second pick with the hope he could stay healthy over the course of a long NHL season and develop quickly.

Dallas, which had the third pick, took defenseman Miro Heiskanen of Finland, followed by Colorado, which took defenseman Cale Makar, who had zoomed up the draft boards after an outstanding season playing in the Alberta Junior League with Brooks. Vancouver was next, and the Canucks took center Elias Peterson from Sweden.

Now it was Vegas' turn.

There were some talented players still on the board. There was Minnesota high school sensation Casey Middlestadt. There was Tri-City forward Michael Rasmussen and centers Gabe Vilardi and Martin Necas.

But the Knights had their eye on Cody Glass, a center from the Portland Winterhawks. He had speed. He had size and he had smarts. He also was 18 years old and he wouldn't have to be rushed in terms of his development.

McPhee kept it short and sweet when he said: "The Vegas Golden Knights select Cody Glass of the Portland Winterhawks."

The first round is one unto itself. And yet it moves fairly quickly. So it wasn't long after the selection of Glass that

McPhee was back up at the podium to announce the Knights had taken Nick Suzuki, a center from the Owen Sound Attack with the No. 13 pick overall. Minutes later, McPhee announced the Knights had selected Erik Brannstrom, a defenseman from Sweden.

The hockey draftniks were quick to heap praise on McPhee and the Knights for the job they did the first day. They loved the Glass pick but they were really enthralled by Brannstrom, who despite being just five feet, nine inches, is a physical player who has great vision and packs a wallop of a shot from the blue line.

Day Two of the entry draft was like a speed dating session. The Knights took nine players between rounds two and seven, starting with Nicolas Hague, a six foot, seven-inch defenseman for the Missassuaga Steelheads. Their other second-round pick was Jake Leschyshyn, a forward for the Regina Pats whose father Curtis played 16 seasons in the NHL.

In all, 12 players were taken over the seven rounds. None would make the inaugural season roster, but McPhee said he was not of the mind to rush his prospects.

"I've never wanted teenagers in the NHL," McPhee said. "I don't think they make you a whole lot better. We have to develop them properly, and we will take our time to do that."

McPhee had plenty of players from which to craft his inaugural roster so he didn't have to bring any of his draftees into the NHL. However, training camp was nine weeks away and lots of work remained to be done, both on and off the ice.

Three days after the entry draft, the Golden Knights held a five-day development camp at the Las Vegas Ice Center on West Flamingo Road. The team's practice facility was still under construction, and while the building was well on its way to completion it wasn't quite ready for hockey.

The majority of the team's draft picks were there along with a lot of free agents. A couple of the expansion draft players were also on the ice, including Alex Tuch.

Tuch had six games of NHL experience after the Minnesota Wild had taken him in the first round of the 2014 entry draft, and the former Boston College star wanted to make an early impression.

Gerard Gallant and his staff were watching from the glass while George McPhee, Kelly McCrimmon and other members of the team's hockey operations staff watched from a perch overlooking the ice. For many of these players, their likely final destination was the Chicago Wolves, who would serve as the American Hockey League affiliate for the Golden Knights.

The rookies who were drafted would all eventually return to their junior teams, or, in Erik Brannstrom's case, play for the senior team in his native Sweden rather than the junior version.

Tuch quickly established himself as one of the best players on the ice. He was strong, confident and smart. He took advantage of the less-than-stellar goaltending that had been assembled. No Marc-Andre Fleurys here. Or Calvin Pickards for that matter.

The daily scrimmages were spirited affairs and fans packed into the small rink to get an early line on who might have a leg up going into training camp in September. It would become a common occurrence once the regular season started, and the team kept its practices open to the general public.

Meanwhile, things were busy off the ice. Season ticket invoices were being sent out, and for the 14,000 who had plunked down their $150 deposits two years before, it was time to pay up or get out.

More than 12,000 stayed with it. Todd Pollock, who now had the title of vice president for ticketing and suites, came up with a plan whereby fans could pick their seats online after having attended an open house at T-Mobile Arena to test-drive their preferred seat locations. Those who paid the most for the longest had priority, and even those who were willing only to give it a shot for the first year still found themselves with good locations from which to choose their seats.

The truth was, even the seats in the upper reaches of T-Mobile Arena were good. You could follow the action with no problem. And if you had issues following the puck, the massive "Knight-tron" video board which hung above center ice gave you a high-resolution look at the action.

For those who didn't buy season tickets and wanted to follow the team, television was their option. The team had announced a deal with AT&T Sportsnet, whose parent company owned DirecTV. The signal for the team, AT&T Sportsnet Rocky Mountain, was supposed to be available in Utah, Wyoming, Colorado, Idaho and Montana along with areas of Southern California, New Mexico and Colorado.

The logic behind choosing AT&T was that the NHL had granted the team territorial rights in those states and owner Bill Foley wanted to take advantage of the opportunity. "We want to be the team of the Rockies," he said.

There were two problems with that. First, the Colorado Avalanche considered itself the team of the Rockies. Second, the channel wasn't available in Las Vegas.

Those who had DirecTV would have the channel. Those who subscribed to a different carrier such as Cox Cable,

CenturyLink's Prism TV or DISH Network would have to rely on their carrier's ability to negotiate a deal to get AT&T Sportsnet on their system. In virtually all cases, it would likely mean an increase in their bill.

It was an angst-filled summer for the fans and in the case of Cox, it didn't get resolved until opening night and just an hour or two before the puck dropped on the team's inaugural game. Prism also worked a deal to get the signal, but DISH and AT&T never did come to an agreement, leaving those subscribers in the dark the entire season.

The team also took a bus promotional tour in August to Utah, Montana and Idaho, which left a number of Las Vegas fans slighted. But the Knights had been doing a number of events in Southern Nevada all along and president Kerry Bubolz wasn't seeing the snub.

What he was seeing was a way to make the in-game experience at T-Mobile Arena something special. This was Las Vegas, after all, and from Bubolz's perspective it needed to be spectacular and fun from the moment you got out of your car to the time you drove home. Win or lose, the plan was to have a good time at a Golden Knights game.

To that end, Bubloz hired Jonny Greco as his director of entertainment. The two had worked together with the NBA's Cleveland Cavaliers and Greco also had worked for WWE Entertainment.

Say what you want about pro wrestling, but the WWE folks know something about getting you out of your seat at its events. Greco was in charge of getting the 17,500 or more fans at T-Mobile Arena on their feet and energized.

The pregame show would be an elaborate mix of sounds, video, music, on-ice entertainment and visuals on the playing surface. Foley had envisioned a moment where the team's mascot — naturally, a Knight — would pull a sword out of a stone, much like King Arthur was able to pry Excalibur free, according to legend.

But as Greco knew from his WWE days, every skit needs a hero and a villain. So before each game, the enemy would approach in the form of a black-draped skater waving the flag of the opposing team that night. At the other end would appear the Golden Knight mascot, who would pull the sword from the stone and ultimately vanquish his enemy.

It was a bit campy but the crowd loved it. It helped fire them up so when the team would hit the ice the roar would be deafening.

There would be cheerleaders. A co-ed ice crew. A drumline. And eventually a second mascot, one that played to kids, a Gila monster named "Chance".

"We want to form traditions, but you can't force it," Greco said. "You can give people some instruction but you can't tell them what to do or it gets annoying. The traditions will come with time."

5. The Season Approaches

The Golden Knights' first training camp was just days away. The temperatures were in the triple digits outside City National Arena. The team's practice facility, which was named after a bank, had purchased the rights. Inside, it was nice and cool. The ice had been put down in both rinks in late July and had been given time to settle and form. They were good and fast sheets that were meant to replicate the ice at T-Mobile Arena.

In the days leading up to the start of camp on September 14, several of the veterans who figured to be on the opening night roster were in town and were working out on their own. There was no rule forcing them to skate. They did it on their own. No coaches. Just the players.

There was speculation as to who would be the team's first captain. As it turned out, the Golden Knights would go without anyone wearing the "C" on their sweater. Instead, a leadership group of veteran players led by Marc-Andre Fleury, Deryk Engelland and James Neal would handle things in the locker room. Six players would serve as alternate captains.

Why not Fleury as captain? The NHL prohibits goaltenders from serving as captains. But there was no doubt who had everyone's attention in the room.

Fleury had a reputation for being a great teammate. He was revered by his fellow Pittsburgh Penguins and endeared himself to the Pittsburgh fans not just for his play on the ice but also for his civic pride off it. He helped establish a Boys and Girls Club in one of the most depressed areas of the city and lent his name and time to many charitable causes.

He was also a bit of a prankster. He was known to pull a fast one on unsuspecting teammates. But it was always in fun and never with malice. His victims couldn't get mad at him. He was their beloved "Flower".

It would be the same with the Golden Knights. Fleury was already a fan favorite and he had settled in to a nice home in Southern Highlands even though most of his teammates chose to live closer to the practice facility in Summerlin.

His roster spot was etched in stone.

And as training camp opened, there wasn't much time to make a positive impression on Gerard Gallant and his coaching staff. His message before his players hit the ice the first day was simple — work hard, play for each other and those who perform the best will play. But most of all, have fun.

The tempo of that first session was ultra-quick and surprisingly sharp. Not a lot of mistakes. Players went from drill to drill seamlessly. Everyone knew their responsibilities and there was not a lot of wasted time. Even the younger players quickly picked things up.

The Knights were supposed to play just six preseason games in order to get ready for their inaugural season. But the NHL asked them to also fly to Vancouver to play the Canucks, who were getting ready to head to China to play the Los Angeles Kings in the first-ever NHL games in that country.

On September 16 at Rogers Arena, they dropped the puck in what was the first-ever game played by the NHL's newest team. The Knights were wearing their white uniforms trimmed in black, gold and red. They also scored first, with Tyler Wong, a free agent rookie forward, scoring 4:58 into the game and becoming the answer to the trivia question: "Who scored the first goal ever for the Golden Knights?"

The Knights went on to a 9-4 victory with Dylan Ferguson getting the win in goal. Ferguson had been acquired shortly after the expansion draft, coming over from Dallas in exchange for Marc Methot. It wouldn't be his last appearance in a Knights uniform.

Two nights later, in Denver, the Knights went to 2-0 beating the Colorado Avalanche 4-1. They suffered their first defeat when they fell 5-2 to San Jose on September 21, but rebounded three nights later with a 4-2 win over Anaheim.

The team's long-awaited home debut came on September 26 against the Los Angeles Kings. Strangely, the Kings had played more games in T-Mobile Arena than the Knights had, having skated twice the year before during the 2016-17 preseason. The game would go to overtime before Brooks Laich was alone in front of Calvin Pickard and scored to give LA a 3-2 win.

The Knights fell again, 4-2 to Colorado on September 28. They were 3-3 for the preseason with one tuneup left. Overall, Gallant was happy with what he had seen so far. The lines were starting to get comfortable working together, the defensive pairings were looking good. Fleury seemed fine in what little time he had played, and while Pickard appeared to be struggling to find a rhythm, his role as Fleury's understudy was already defined and he was fine with it.

Still, there were some reasons for concern. Neal had yet to play in the preseason after he recovered from off-season surgery on his right hand, which he had injured during the Western Conference Finals. And with opening night on October 6 in Dallas against the Stars coming up quick on the calendar, nobody knew if Neal would be in the lineup.

The other concern was Vadim Shipachyov. The Russian center was struggling to adjust to the NHL and he was not producing. Gallant was playing Shipachyov with Reilly Smith and Jonathan Marchessault, hoping the two former Florida Panthers would connect with their linemate. But it was quickly becoming evident that the Shipachyov the team's scouts had seen play in Russia and the Shipachyov they were watching in Las Vegas wasn't the same player. Something wasn't right.

The Knights' final preseason game was scheduled for October 1 at T-Mobile Arena against San Jose. For Shipachyov, it would be one final opportunity to prove to Gallant he belonged in the opening night lineup. For Las Vegas, it would be a day the city would never forget.

6. A City Hurts

It was a normal Sunday the morning of October 1. The high temperature was expected to be 90 degrees. There had been a few passing clouds but nothing to get concerned over.

People went about their business in the usual fashion. Many opted for brunch at their favorite local establishment. The sports books were jammed as always with fans watching the National Football League. People walked their dogs, went jogging, sipped coffee or buried their faces in the screens of their cellphones, the new national pastime.

For the Golden Knights, the day meant the final preseason game. The San Jose Sharks were in town and the game had a 5 p.m. start, which would turn out to be a significant thing. The Sharks had already beaten the Knights in San Jose, but as any coach will tell you, preseason wins don't mean a thing.

Gerard Gallant was still juggling his lines and his defensive pairings, trying to hit on the right combinations. He thought he had the components of his first line established with Jonathan Marchessault and Reilly Smith. But he still needed the right person to center the trio. He was hoping Vadim Shipachyov would be that person but things didn't appear to be panning out. Oscar Lindberg, who had been a serviceable center with

65

the New York Rangers, appeared to be a better option at this point.

Meanwhile, Cody Eakin, who was looking to bounce back from an injury-plagued year with the Dallas Stars, was the second line center for the time being. Gallant had veteran winger David Perron with Eakin and the thinking was that when James Neal was ready, he would join the line.

Erik Haula was the third line center and he had a variety of wingers skating with him. Brendan Leipsic skated with Haula as did rookie Alex Tuch, who was trying to make the team.

The fourth line was Pierre-Edouard Bellemare skating with Tomas Nosek. Will Carrier would eventually become a permanent fixture on that line, but for the final preseason game, Carrier was scratched and William Karlsson was taking his place.

Karlsson was a natural center but he could also play on the wing. He was one of the smarter players on the roster and one of the most adaptable. He never seemed flustered or frustrated.

On defense, the separation was much clearer. Derek Engelland was going to be playing on opening night. So was Luca Sbisa, the veteran acquired from the Canucks in the expansion draft. Nate Schmidt and Colin Miller were also looking like they would be on the flight to Dallas in a few days. Both had the ability to skate and join the rush and were adept at supporting the attack. Miller possessed the hardest shot of anyone on the roster. He won the hardest shot competition at the AHL All-Star Game a few years before he made it to the Boston Bruins. And while he was sometimes a defensive liability, Miller was working with assistant coach Ryan McGill to shore up those deficiencies.

As the afternoon wore on, it was becoming a busy day on the Las Vegas Strip. Not only was T-Mobile Arena hosting hockey, a couple of blocks away across from the Mandalay Bay Hotel and Casino, the Route 91 Harvest Country Music Festival was cranking up for its third and final day in Las Vegas.

Las Vegas has always been a place for entertainers to perform. Elvis Presley became his own cottage industry during the 1960s and '70s with his regular appearances. Every major music act, from the Beatles to Bruce Springsteen had shown up to play Vegas.

Country music was no exception. And while Las Vegas wasn't Nashville, it was still a popular place for that genre of entertainers to play. And the Route 91 Festival was no exception. It had come to town in 2014 and this year's lineup included Eric Church, Sam Hunt, Jake Owen, Lee Brice and Jason Aldean.

A couple of the Golden Knights players and staff members had attended the Friday and Saturday performances. Some talked about going back for the Sunday show after the game. With a 5 p.m. puck drop, there would be enough time to get over to the concert site and catch Aldean, who was scheduled to close out the show.

There were 16,479 inside T-Mobile for the final preseason contest, a game which saw Haula score at 8:08 of the first period to give the Knights a 1-0 lead. The Sharks would answer with three goals against Marc-Andre Fleury before the Knights rallied with goals by Perron and Miller to tie it 3-3 going into the third period.

But Nick DeSimone scored midway through the third period for San Jose and an empty-net goal from Joel Ward with 28 seconds remaining sealed a 5-3 win for the Sharks and a 3-4 preseason record for the Knights. The game ended at 7:40 p.m. and the fans filed out somewhat disappointed that their team had lost but buoyed by the fact that there was some talent here and this might not be your typical expansion team.

Maybe they could win a few more games than the experts were predicting. Heck, maybe they might be able to sneak into the playoffs if everything broke right.

Some of the players headed down the street to The Cosmopolitan hotel for a post-game dinner. Over steaks, fish, wine and beer, they would talk about what had transpired to date and what Gallant might do to get his lines set for Friday's opener against Dallas.

Calvin Pickard thought about going back to the Route 91 Festival. After all, he didn't play against the Sharks and he had been there the first two nights. But Pickard decided at the last minute to grab something to eat and head home.

Meanwhile, down the street across from Mandalay Bay, the concert was well under way. Thousands were enjoying the music. Everyone appeared to be enjoying themselves. The sun had come down and the weather had cooled. It was a near-perfect evening.

For one person across the street, it was a little too perfect.

Stephen Paddock lived 90 miles away from the Strip in Mesquite, a town that bordered Nevada and Utah. He had done well for himself in real estate and he liked to gamble. He was 64 years old and he looked like he could have been your next-door neighbor.

Paddock had driven to Las Vegas and checked into Mandalay Bay a few days prior to the weekend. He had a room on the 32nd floor facing the Strip and the concert site across the street. Nothing seemed unusual about that.

But he made several trips from the garage to his room with several bags and items. But even that didn't set off any red flags.

It was now after 10 p.m. Jason Aldean had taken the stage and he was performing for the approximately 22,000 who had stuck around to watch him and his band. Paddock was also watching … and waiting.

He had set up a mini-arsenal in his room with rifles that had been converted into automatic weapons with the use of a device called a bumpstock. He could fire off hundreds of rounds in seconds.

At 10:05 p.m., Paddock began to shoot. At first, no one was sure if it was something connected to the show. Perhaps fireworks? But it quickly became evident this had nothing to do with the concert. This was a deranged gunman turned loose on an unsuspecting, defenseless crowd.

As the bullets continued to rain down, people ran for cover. But for many, there was nowhere to hide. They were caught in a hailstorm of gunfire. Bodies were dropping everywhere.

Police and hotel security were attempting to get to the shooter. Meanwhile, Paddock continued his assault, emptying clip after clip. Ten minutes later, it was over. Paddock had taken his own life, and across the street, dozens were dead and hundreds more injured.

It was mass confusion, up and down the Strip. Most hotels and casinos went into lockdown. At T-Mobile Arena, a few journalists who were finishing up were also denied exiting the building.

There were rumors of a terrorist attack. On social media, erroneous information was being put out. Nobody was sure what to believe.

For the Golden Knights players who were dining at the Cosmopolitan Hotel, they would remain there for the next three hours. People were on their phones, trying to find out from others just what was going on.

Meanwhile, the team was quickly taking roll call. Every player, coach, staff member and team official was contacted, and they confirmed their whereabouts. Pickard had made the right decision not to go to the show.

Back at the concert site, the dead and the wounded were being attended to. There were countless acts of heroism as many risked their own lives to help others. Every hospital in the city was on red alert as sirens blared with ambulances, police and emergency vehicles racing to and fro.

A day, which began tranquil and peaceful, much like New York had on the morning of September 11, 2001, or Oklahoma City had on April 19, 1995, had ended in horror and tragedy.

The Golden Knights had a hockey game to play in five days.

Suddenly, that wasn't so important.

7. A City Heals

The images on television were undeniable. The carnage was unimaginable. They began counting the dead and trying to account for the wounded. Twelve. Then 20. Then 32. Eventually, the number of dead in the Route 91 Harvest Music Festival attack had reached 58. The number of wounded were over 500. How many exactly, no one was sure yet.

Las Vegas, as a city, was numb. How could one person cause all this? Why would Stephen Paddock do what he did? The people wanted answers, and Sheriff Joe Lombardo was doing his best to provide those answers.

Meanwhile, in Summerlin the Golden Knights were preparing to practice at City National Arena. Other than Deryk Engelland, none of them had lived in Las Vegas. This was still a new place for them. When the expansion draft had wrapped up, Engelland and his wife Melissa served as unofficial concierges for the defenseman's new teammates and their families. Need a place to go shopping? Call Melissa. Looking for a church? Deryk might know someone. From a restaurant for dinner or a park to take the kids to play, if you needed help or a recommendation, you called the Engellands.

Now their new city was one in mourning. The full impact of what had taken place still hadn't hit them. But they also knew that they were now part of something big, whether they liked it or not.

Las Vegas' NHL team was going to play an important role in helping the city heal. There was no getting around it.

But how? How can a group of hockey players help?

When it was appropriate, the players would get out into the community. They would meet with the first responders who put their own lives on the line to save others. They would get to the hospitals, meet with the wounded and encourage them to get well. They would visit the local blood banks, where hundreds were lined up for hours waiting to donate.

Team officials quickly organized groups of players to make the requisite visits. By Tuesday they were out all over the city, posing for pictures, signing autographs, having a few private words with those who needed their support the most.

"Sports are a great thing. It can help take people's minds off of things," defenseman Nate Schmidt said. "As much as the city has embraced us, we're a part of Las Vegas."

For Engelland, trying to make sense of it all was an exercise in futility.

"My wife is still shaken up. She's almost scared to go to the games, to take the kids to the home opener," he said. "It hits hard and it hits in a lot of different ways. You see these things happen all over the world and no one ever thinks it's going to happen in their backyard. For it to happen here, it's horrific."

After meeting with the first responders, Jonathan Marchessault was left with a healthy dose of humility.

"We're nothing compared to those guys," Marchessault said. "What they've done and what they do for our community and our country, it's amazing. If you think about it we're just entertainers. That's it. They save lives. They make sure everything goes properly around us. They're survivors. They're warriors."

And while this was going on, the team had to prepare for its opener on Friday. When they stepped onto the ice now, it was with a different sense of purpose. They were no longer just playing for themselves. They weren't just playing for their fans. They were playing for an entire city. Gallant's message of coming to the rink every day and having fun suddenly felt conflicted. Here was their city grieving, and yet they had a job to do, which was to entertain.

As the players prepared for the historic opener in Dallas, the marketing side had a dilemma on its hands. Elaborate plans had been in the works for a couple of months to celebrate the team's home opener on October 10 at T-Mobile Arena. It was to be a festive affair, one of fun and all sorts of surprises. NHL commissioner Gary Bettman planned to attend as did local officials.

Suddenly, that celebration did not seem appropriate. The team had a Fan Fest scheduled for October 3 downtown at the Fremont Street Experience, which was to kick off the season. That was put on hold indefinitely. The attack was still fresh in everyone's mind. No way could the hockey team expect its fans to show up and cheer the coming of the inaugural season.

That was the easy one. The pregame celebration for October 10 was far more problematic. The team had to do a 180-degree turn and make the celebration respectful, and with a somber tone to it.

Kim Frank, the team's vice president of marketing and her staff along with Brian Killingsworth, the team's chief marketing officer, met at City National Arena. Kerry Bubolz took part in the meetings along with Jonny Greco, who was going to coordinate whatever pregame activities there were going to be.

While the front office sorted out the details for the home opener, the Knights boarded their plane for Dallas. McPhee had made some tough decisions following the final preseason game. He had to turn in his roster to the league and when he did, some noticeable names were missing.

Calvin Pickard was no longer with the team. His preseason struggles combined with picking up Malcolm Subban off waivers sealed his fate. Picard was traded to Toronto for forward Tobias Lindberg and a sixth-round draft pick in 2018. Subban, the younger brother of Nashville Predators all-star defenseman P.K. Subban, was considered a talented prospect. He was just 24 years old and had lots of upside. The feeling was that goaltending coach David Prior would be able to work with Subban and accelerate his development. Besides, Fleury was going to play the majority of the games and Subban wouldn't need to be rushed.

On defense, Shea Theodore was headed to the Chicago Wolves while Clayton Stoner was put on injured reserve. Theodore had shown some ability offensively during the preseason, but defensively he was still trying to find his way. Rather than make him a healthy scratch, better for him to play regular minutes in the AHL.

Clayton Stoner reportedly had sustained an abdominal injury similar to one that had limited him to just 14 games with Anaheim in 2016-17. He would never play a game for the Golden Knights.

Alex Tuch also was headed to the AHL. While his game was good, there was no spot for him, and like Theodore,

McPhee felt Tuch would be better served playing in Chicago than sitting in a press box with the Knights.

But the biggest, most shocking move was Vadim Shipachyov. The player the Knights hoped would center their first line had failed to deliver and he too was optioned to the Chicago Wolves. But unlike Tuch and Theodore who had accepted their reassignments gracefully and reported with no issues, Shipachyov balked at being sent to the minors. No way did he want to leave his family in Las Vegas to go work in yet another strange city. He and his wife were still struggling to deal with the October 1 shootings and how uncomfortable they were. So the last thing he wanted was to accept a demotion.

He was getting paid nine million dollars to play hockey and from McPhee's perspective, it was a case of "If we're paying you, you're playing where we tell you to."

Shipachyov reluctantly agreed to report to the Wolves, who, ironically, were also starting their season in Texas against the Texas Stars. However, he refused to suit up and play.

It was the kind of distraction the Golden Knights didn't need, particularly as they were trying to focus on their first-ever game. But the team's leadership group made sure it didn't impact the locker room. Everyone was excited about playing in the historic opener and coach Gerard Gallant's lineup for October 6, 2017, looked like this:

Forward lines:
Reilly Smith-Oscar Lindberg-Jonathan Marchessault
David Perron-Cody Eakin-James Neal

Brendan Leipsic-Erik Haula-William Karlsson
Tomas Nosek-Pierre-Edouard Bellemare-Will Carrier

Defense pairs:
Deryk Engelland-Jason Garrison
Colin Miller-Brayden McNabb
Nate Schmidt-Luca Sbisa
Goaltenders
Marc-Andre Fleury
Malcolm Subban

The Stars were aware of what had transpired in Las Vegas, and their organization was also dealing with the loss of a loved one. Team broadcaster Dave Strader had fought a brave battle against bile duct cancer and died on October 1. The team was going to honor Strader on the night of their opener. Now they would also honor the 58 shooting victims in Las Vegas.

As the Knights players stood on their blue line for the pregame ceremony, the Stars joined them, standing behind the visitors in a show of solidarity. A video tribute for Strader was shown inside American Airlines Center and was met with warm applause. Then a moment of silence for both Strader and the shooting victims was observed. It was a nice touch by the NHL and Stars management.

The game would be televised back to Las Vegas as an eleventh-hour deal had been struck between AT&T, which owned AT&T Sportsnet Rocky Mountain, and Cox Communications, the largest cable distributor in the area. And as the puck dropped at 7:42 p.m. in Dallas, the Golden Knights were officially playing hockey that would count in the NHL standings.

The Stars were coming in waves, outworking the Knights and putting pressure on Fleury. But despite 14 shots on goal and several missed quality chances, the game remained scoreless heading into the second period. But eventually Dallas solved Fleury as Tyler Seguin scored the game's first goal with just under three minutes to play in the second period.

It was 1-0 with 20 minutes to play. Yet despite being outshot 35-18 over the first two periods, the Knights believed they were in good shape. Dallas starting goaltender Ben Bishop had to leave the game in the second period with an injury after he took a shot to the face and had to go to concussion protocol. Kari Lehtonen, his backup, had struggled mightily the year before and now Lehtonen was being asked to hold the fort.

The Knights picked up the pace in the third period and James Neal scored the franchise's first regular-season goal, a wrist shot as he had jumped on the ice as an extra attacker on a delayed penalty to the Stars.

Neal had missed the entire preseason as his surgically repaired right hand was still healing and he was a game-time decision for opening night. But he convinced Gallant he was good to go, and he delivered with 9:33 to play to tie the game at 1-1. The goal had given the Knights a lift and they continued to press forward, working hard on the forecheck and putting additional pressure on the Stars' defense and their vulnerable goalie.

With under three minutes to play and overtime looming, it was Neal again delivering. Garrison had gotten the puck out of the Knights' end to Eakin who skated down the middle. Neal, who was moving down the right side in support of the play, caught Eakin's eye. He slid the puck to Neal and while it wasn't a perfect pass, it was close enough. And as Neal lost his balance, he still was able to make a play, shooting from one knee from inside the right face-off circle. Lehtonen was slow to respond and the Knights suddenly were in front 2-1.

Fleury took over from there, repelling the Stars' attempts to tie it late, and when the game was over, the Knights swarmed their goaltender and hugged each other. The franchise had won its first game and there was excitement stemming from the victorious locker room.

"I expected to stop them all," Fleury said after stopping 45 of the 46 shots he faced. "But it's a great win for us. We're a new team and everyone kept working hard. It's exciting to win the first game."

Gallant said of the historic first win: "We worked hard all game. We stuck around, we got a couple of good opportunities and we capitalized on them."

But the Knights had little time to celebrate. They were flying to Phoenix to face the Arizona Coyotes the next night in Glendale, at Gila River Arena. The Coyotes were a struggling franchise and were trying to move on without their captain and spiritual leader, Shane Doan, who had retired after the 2016-17 season. They had changed coaches, replacing Dave Tippett with Rick Tocchet. They had also traded popular goalie Mike Smith to Calgary, and this was a team that was in transition.

Once again, the Knights found themselves trailing as Tobias Reider had scored 5:52 into the game. But unlike the opener where the home team carried the play, the visitors were the ones dominating. The Knights pressured Antti Raanta with 32 shots over the first two periods yet they still trailed 1-0 heading into the third period. Fleury was equally brilliant in the Vegas net, denying several quality chances by the Coyotes and also getting help from the goalpost and crossbar on a couple of occasions.

But the Knights were still unable to score and time was running out. With 1:12 to play, Nate Schmidt finally broke through, tying the game with a shot from the slot. It went to overtime and once again Neal delivered, scoring the game-winner with 1:14 to play after David Perron had set him up on the right side.

"You have to play a patient, simple game and wait for your chances," Neal said. "I think that's what we did."

Though the season was only two games old, the Knights were showing a trait associated with winners — resiliency.

"Nobody was panicking on the bench," Schmidt said. "We were getting our chances. It was just a matter of getting one to go in."

They were undefeated and going home to what would be an emotional night, the kind of night none of them would ever forget.

8. "Vegas Strong"

The Golden Knights were 2-0 when they returned to Las Vegas for their October 10 historic home opener. The Arizona Coyotes were the scheduled opponent. But the one thought on everyone's minds was, "What would the pregame ceremony be?"

The team had already made adjustments on the fly, changing almost three months worth of work and planning into a new ceremony in about a week. NHL commissioner Gary Bettman was still planning to attend, and he acknowledged that this would not be your normal inaugural home game.

"Plans that we're on the drawing board to celebrate the first regular-season game have been modified out of respect due to the terrible tragedy," Bettman said. "What will take place will be in the spirit of what I believe sports teams mean to a community — bringing people together in a sense of unity."

General manager George McPhee, who was kept in the loop on the ceremony plans, said, "It's not going to be a typical opener — we will save that for Friday (October 13). Tuesday night is not about us. It's about honoring and remembering the victims, supporting their families and recognizing the first responders who did tremendous work."

It was a tough task. Could they pull it off?

The game was being televised on the NBC Sports Network, so the entire country was going to see the ceremony. At the morning skate the players tried to keep their focus on hockey, but they knew this was going to be a special night.

"There are going to be a lot of emotions," Deryk Engelland said. "Because of the tragedy, I don't know if words can describe how emotional it will be ... We have to do our part to help this city past this whole ordeal."

And while Las Vegas was still trying to deal with what happened October 1, majority owner Bill Foley was dealing with his own personal crisis. A series of wildfires was sweeping through Northern California and were approaching the vineyards near Napa and Sonoma, where Foley's winemaking business was located. The fires had already done considerable damage and were now threatening Foley's property.

"It's horrible what's going on up there," Foley said. "But we're hoping everything will be all right."

Wine is a billion-dollar industry in that region, and Foley also had hundreds of employees at risk. Evacuations were ordered in the area and all anyone could do was hope and pray the flames passed them by.

Those prayers were answered. Foley's vineyards were spared. All his employees were safe. One person lost his home to the fires but everyone else's property remained intact.

"We were extremely lucky," he said. "The fires missed us."

Not everyone in the area was as fortunate. Forty-four people died, 245,000 acres were wiped out, and 8,900 buildings were damaged or destroyed. The estimated cost from the fires was $9.4 billion.

Back in Las Vegas, the fact the team had gotten off to a fast start was not lost on either the players or the fans. The players wanted to win this game, not only for the city, but to sustain the early positive momentum they had managed to establish in their brief existence. It was two points in the standings, but those two points counted just as much in mid-October as they would in early April.

As the gates opened to T-Mobile Arena, there was a mixed vibe of excited anticipation and a tinge of dread. There would be hockey played, but those who were in attendance would be part of paying their respects for the 58 who had died in the attack and supporting the hundreds more who were wounded. It would also be an opportunity to say "Thank You" to the first responders who acted swiftly and courageously.

The team had gotten permission from the NHL to embed the names of the 58 victims into the ice. It was a wonderful tribute. But it was only the beginning. The team had replaced the advertising on the dasher boards with the message "VEGAS STRONG", which became the catchphrase the city had rallied around. The players wore a white, gold and black stick on the back of their helmets, which had an outline of the state of Nevada with a silhouetted skyline of the Strip, the team's secondary crossed-swords logo and the words "Vegas Strong" above.

Shortly after 7:15 p.m. the lights were dimmed. As orchestral music played, the Knights' players and coaches were introduced. One by one, they were accompanied by a police officer, a firefighter, a doctor, a nurse, a paramedic — the real heroes. In a symbolic gesture, the honorees stood on the Golden Knights' blue line, the players and coaches standing behind them. It was hard to tell who was enjoying the moment more, the players or the first responders.

In all, 26 were publicly honored. They were:

Firefighter Ben Kole; Firefighter Derek Sutherland; Registered Nurse Joe Bruno; Doctor Jung-Taek Yoon; Sergeant William Matchko; Paramedic Sheri Jones; Registered Nurse Brad Skilling; Firefighter Ryan Nimmo; Engineer James Lobrovich; Doctor Syed Saquib; EMT Nick Pedulla; Doctor Carl Williams; Sergeant Stuart Richmond; Registered Nurse Sindy Namnakani; Registered Nurse Sarita Lundin; K9 officer Dave Newton; Registered Nurse Staci Sei; Firefighter Tyler McFate; Dispatcher Andrew Jones; Registered Nurse Tiffinee Fontain; Paramedic Aaron Goldstein; Officer Tyler Peterson; Firefighter Ryan Haberman; SWAT officer Levi Hancock; Sergeant Josh Bitsko and Clark County Fire Captain Doniel Leak.

There was a special ceremonial puck drop which included survivors of the attack along with Foley and Clark County Commissioner Steve Sisolak, in whose district the shooting had taken place.

Then there were 58 seconds of silence to honor the victims with their names projected on the ice. The Coyotes had joined the Golden Knights' players on the blue line behind the first responders. The Dallas Stars had performed a similar gesture on opening night a few days before and it was a classy move on the Arizona players' part.

Following the performance of the national anthem, which was done by performers from the Route 91 Festival, there was a speech to be given.

It wasn't from Bettman, Foley, Sisolak or any other politician. Deryk Engelland would deliver a brief but heartfelt message.

Engelland wasn't a world-class speaker. He didn't have Nate Schmidt's glibness or Marc-Andre Fleury's folksy way of chatting. He was a down-to-earth, straightforward guy. Ask him a question, he would answer it the best he could, quietly and professionally. You never heard anything controversial come out of Engelland's mouth.

Now he was about to speak words that would resonate with the franchise and the city forever. And as he skated to center ice and took the microphone, Engelland surveyed the scene. Then he began to speak:

"Like all of you, I am proud to call Las Vegas home. I met my wife here. My kids were born here. And I know how special this city is. To all the brave first responders that have worked tirelessly and courageously throughout this whole tragedy, we thank you. To the families and friends of the victims, know we will do everything we can to help you and our city heal.

"We are Vegas Strong."

It was both brief and beautiful. Fitting words for a fitting end to a fitting ceremony. In the T-Mobile press box where reporters were wiping away tears, they were quickly getting Engelland's message out on social media.

The consensus was that the Knights had done a marvelous job. Not only was it tastefully done, it had hit all the right chords. As George McPhee said the day before, this was about the victims and the first responders, not about the hockey team.

"It was a powerful moment," Foley said of the ceremony. "It's a process here. It's a tough deal that happened nine days ago, but we're trying to do our part. Our players are really trying to do their part."

Now it was time to play. And the crowd quickly shifted moods from respectful to excited. "Go Knights Go!" chants rang out throughout the building as referee Dave Jackson dropped the puck at 7:45 p.m.

These two teams had met three nights before in Glendale, Arizona, and the Coyotes had outplayed the Knights for the most part. It took a Herculean effort by Fleury in the Vegas net to keep his team in the game and they would win 2-1 in overtime as James Neal scored the game-winner.

This night, the Knights would be the team with the jump. They swarmed the Coyotes, forechecking fiercely, taking the body at every turn, getting the fans engaged as they fired shot after shot at Antti Raanta, the Arizona goaltender. Then, 2:31 into the game, Tomas Nosek was set up by Pierre-Edouard Bellemare after Luca Sbisa had done a good job keeping the puck in the Coyotes' zone at the blue line. Nosek was unchecked and he put it past Raanta to give the Knights an early 1-0 lead.

The crowd was going nuts. All this pent-up energy was now being unleashed as the noise level increased. Somehow, it got even louder when Brendan Leipsic got the puck to Engelland, who was at the right point. Engelland unleashed a slap shot and the puck whizzed by Raanta for a 2-0 lead.

It was the kind of moment Hollywood, or Disney, in particular, would dream of. The man who only a few minutes before said, "We are Vegas Strong", had delivered again. But the Knights were only getting started.

Neal, the hero of the first two wins, scored less than two minutes after Engelland to make it 3-0. Midway through the period, Neal delivered again to make it 4-0 and chase Raanta from the Arizona net.

The Knights would go on to win 5-2 and improve to 3-0. Afterward, they talked about the ceremony, about coming through at home ice for their crowd and how they hoped their performance would help the city heal.

"The response from the crowd was phenomenal," Engelland said. "It was the least we could do for those people that went through all that. We want to get every win we can for the city and the people that were involved.

"When you get texts from the fire department, saying the spirits are lifting around the department, it's crazy."

Neal said he was honored to be part of history.

"This was the game I wanted to play in," he said. "I didn't know if I would make it to Dallas or Arizona. But I pointed to this game. I wanted to play in the first home game."

Coach Gerard Gallant said: "We talked about tonight being the most important game we'll ever play. We're playing for our city, for the tragedy that happened, for all the people that were here tonight and were affected by the tragedy. I thought the guys did a hell of a job."

9. The Fall Of Flower

The Golden Knights were 3-0, playing well and establishing their identity as a hard-working team that was resilient and one that got along with each other.

The schedule called for the team to be home for seven straight games. October 13 would be the second of those seven and the Detroit Red Wings would be the opponent.

While the pregame ceremony for October 10 was muted and subdued, the pregame ceremony for October 13 would be far more celebratory. It would be the debut of the originally planned pregame show, complete with the Golden Knight vanquishing the evil adversary. It would also be the unveiling of a second mascot, a Gila monster named "Chance". The idea was to have a mascot that kids could relate to, although at first not everyone was sure what to make of Chance.

The team's cheerleaders, the Golden Aces, also made their debut. They were young, attractive ladies dressed in medieval outfits that bared far more skin than anything a fair maiden wore during the Middle Ages. But the outfits were tastefully done, and they were accompanied by a drumline that would perform during games in front of a "castle" located behind the goal.

The team's in-game hosts, Strip performer Mark Shunock and country music radio DJ Big D, were charged with cranking up the energy level in T-Mobile Arena and they were good at it.

The Red Wings were one of the NHL's "Original Six" teams and were very popular. They had a lot of fans in Southern Nevada, not the least of whom was Derek Stevens, who owned the D Las Vegas Hotel and Casino downtown.

Stevens was one of the first casino owners to support the Golden Knights venture, cutting a deal with the team to host watch parties for home and away games and stage a "Fan Fest" at various junctures of the season, where the team and its fans could intermingle and celebrate together.

He was also a hard-core Red Wings fan. Stevens was old enough to remember Gerard Gallant when he played for the Wings and was witness to Detroit's four Stanley Cup championships in the late 1990s and into the 2000s.

But as much as Stevens loved the Wings, he loved the Golden Knights more. However, there were a few thousand who weren't as conflicted when it came to where their loyalties laid. They wore their red jerseys as they entered T-Mobile Arena and it would be a sign of things to come throughout the season.

When people paid for their season tickets, what they did with them was their business. If someone wanted to sell his or her seats to any of the online secondary ticket brokers, there wasn't much, if anything, the team could do about it. And with the NHL schedule having come out in late June, opposing fans had plenty of time to plan a trip to Las Vegas, book a flight, a hotel and, of course, find tickets.

It ticked off owner Bill Foley that so many people would see an opportunity to help pay for their season ticket bill, which was a substantial financial investment, by selling their seats to the enemy's fans. But what could he do?

There was a much different energy in the building on Oct. 13 as the puck was dropped. It felt normal, as if the events of October 1 had never happened. However, during every game there would be a reminder of that horrific night as the team honored an individual, be it a surviving victim, a first responder or someone else who was involved. With it would come the requisite standing ovation from the crowd, even from the visiting team's fans.

The Red Wings were holding a 2-1 lead in the second period when Anthony Mantha, Detroit's big power forward, bore down on Fleury with defenseman Luca Sbisa trying to catch him. Sbisa shoved Mantha from behind and the six foot, five inch Mantha collided with Fleury, his knee catching the goaltender in the head.

Fleury was face down on the ice as Kyle Moore, the team's associate head trainer, came to his aid. The goaltender was woozy, but he insisted on staying in the game.

The NHL has observers at every game so that when contact with a player's head is made, league officials are supposed to determine whether or not the player should leave the game and undergo concussion protocol. It means heading to the locker room for a series of cognitive tests. If the player passes, he can return to the game upon the approval of physicians.

In this case, Fleury was not required to leave the game. And when the second period ended, his team was in front 3-2. Between the second and third periods, another battery of tests were administered. Fleury apparently passed them because when the third period began he was in goal for the Golden Knights.

But something wasn't right. He was a bit tentative moving in his crease. The Red Wings tied it. Then they went ahead 4-3 on Frans Nielsen's goal at the 7:03 mark. The Red Wings beat Fleury two more times and went on to a 6-3 victory.

The Knights were undefeated no more. But they had a far bigger issue to deal with. What was believed to be a sore neck for Fleury was now determined to be a concussion.

Fleury had suffered two previous concussions while he was with the Pittsburgh Penguins, and he missed substantial playing time in both cases. The question for the team now was, how long would he be out?

"The next day, that's when everything hit me: The headaches, dizziness and blurred vision," Fleury said. "Then I knew, that was it."

Fleury went to a couple of different neurologists and the diagnosis was the same — he had a concussion, and he had to stay off the ice.

"On the hit, I felt neck pain that was bothering me a lot," Fleury said. "I told the trainer I was fine because it was just neck pain. Then in the third period, it started to get a little worse. My neck was the thing that bothered me the most, and I thought I could play with it and finish the game. Looking back, maybe I should have pulled myself."

The days stretched into weeks, then months. There was speculation Fleury might retire, though he said it never crossed his mind.

Meanwhile, who was going to play in Fleury's place? They had traded Calvin Pickard. Malcolm Subban, who was Fleury's current backup, had only a couple of games of NHL experience. He was still trying to figure things out, working with goaltending coach David Prior every day.

Maybe George McPhee could swing a trade for a more experienced goalie. He looked into it, then decided not to break up his roster for what he hoped would be a short-term fix.

Two days later, the Knights hosted the Boston Bruins, Subban's former team. And it was Subban who got the nod. To back up Subban, Maxime Lagace was recalled from the AHL. League was no more ready to play than Subban, but there he was, on the bench, a Knights baseball cap on his head as Subban led the team onto the T-Mobile Arena ice.

Fleury wasn't the only player hurt against the Red Wings. Both Jonathan Marchessault and Erik Haula had sustained lower-body injuries and both were out of the lineup. Taking one of their places was Alex Tuch, who had been recalled from the Chicago Wolves, where he had scored four goals in five games.

The other replacement? Vadim Shipachyov. "Shippy", as everyone called him, had last played on October 1. But here was his chance to make a positive impression and maybe get back in McPhee's good graces.

Ironically, both Tuch and Shipachyov would score in the second period, giving the Knights a 2-0 lead. Subban was looking good in the Vegas net and resembled an NHL goalie. He was working on a shutout with a minute to go when David Pastrnak beat him with 30 seconds to go to cut it to 2-1. But Oscar Lindberg scored into an empty net 16 seconds later to seal the 3-1 win.

"I thought I played pretty good," Subban said of his performance and his first NHL victory. "The biggest thing was my depth and not getting too deep in the net. Give myself the better opportunity to make the save. I feel like I did that.

"There weren't too many high chances. A lot of textbook saves and just having good rebound control. I'm happy to get the win."

Boston coach Bruce Cassidy said his team could have made Subban work a little harder.

"We know Malcolm well, and he is a good first-shot goaltender," Cassidy said. "We wanted to put some stress on him with the second ones and I don't think we did a very good job."

The Knights had bounced back from their first defeat and played well in doing so. They built on the Boston win by beating Buffalo in overtime 5-4 in what was a wild affair. The Knights had a 4-1 lead 3:50 into the third period, only to see the Sabres rally to tie it 4-4 with nine seconds to go, as Evander Kane beat Subban from in-close. But with 1:08 to play in overtime, David Perron's goal won it.

St. Louis was in town on October 21 and Subban's confidence appeared to be growing. He was 2-0 as the Knights' starting goalie, and despite giving up a goal midway through the first period, he didn't appear rattled.

With the Knights ahead 2-1 in the third period, the Blues' Jaden Schwartz had a close-in opportunity that appeared to be ticketed for the corner. Subban slid across to his right and managed to get his right pad on the shot. But in doing so, he appeared to have injured his leg. He was helped off the ice and Oscar Dansk, who had been called up from the AHL to serve as the backup while Lagace was returned to the Wolves, was making his NHL debut with nine minutes to play.

Dansk had played in one of the preseason games against Colorado and had played okay. But he was very much an unknown quantity. All the 17,883 spectators inside T-Mobile knew was that their team was now playing its third goalie in four games and in the back of their minds the question was, "Just what the hell was going on here?"

The Blues tied it 2-2 on Alex Pietrangelo's goal with 5:08 to play and for the second straight game it went into overtime. But once again the Knights prevailed, this time thanks to William Karlsson, who scored with 24 seconds left after Reilly Smith hit him in stride with a perfect pass on a 2-on-1, and Karlsson one-timed it past Carter Hutton.

It was the first goal of the year for Karlsson, who was now playing more minutes with Marchessault out as he joined Smith and Lindberg on the top line.

Karlsson had looked at Vegas as an opportunity for a fresh start. He had been a fourth-line player at Columbus and had just six goals and 19 assists in 2016-17. But he was a smart player who had a quick release and knew how to get himself open. He also was a very good defensive forward who was reliable in his own end and wasn't afraid to sacrifice offense if it meant shutting down the opposition. In other words, he was Gerard Gallant's kind of player.

The next day, the news regarding Subban wasn't good. He had a lower-body injury and would be out indefinitely. Now McPhee really had a dilemma on his hands. Everyone was calling for him to make a move, acquire an experienced goalie ASAP. Fleury wasn't close to being ready to return to work. Now his backup was out.

Instead, McPhee stood pat. He would ride it out with Dansk and Lagace, who had been recalled yet again from Chicago and was starting to rack up some pretty good frequent-flier miles. McPhee was reluctant to break up what was starting to shape up as a successful roster, one that was developing some good chemistry while showing some ability to win games, be it coming from behind or finding a way to hold on.

The Knights wrapped up their first home-stand by beating Chicago 4-2, then shutting out Colorado 7-0. Marchessault and Haula were back in the lineup. Marchessault returned against the Blackhawks, Haula against the Avalanche, and both scored in the shutout win over Colorado while Dansk was in net for both wins.

The Knights were an amazing 8-1 and were challenging for the top spot in the Pacific Division. How could an expansion team be this good so soon? Some thought it was just beginner's luck, and there was no way they could keep it going, especially playing with a third-string goalie.

But what people didn't know was that David Prior had worked with both Dansk and Lagace during the team's development camp back in late June, and he saw something in both goalies. As a result, he felt he could improve Dansk and Lagace sufficiently enough to make them NHL-ready.

He reported that to McPhee, who, as he had shown in other instances, trusted the word of his staff. If Prior said the team would be all right playing the two kids while waiting for Fleury and Subban to get back on the ice, McPhee would side with Prior's assessment of the situation. And while the temptation to do something had to be strong, something else inside him was saying, "Don't do anything."

That patience would be severely tested in a few days.

The Knights had already shown an ability to win away from Las Vegas, having been successful in Dallas and Arizona. But the team now faced its first true test of being able to handle the road.

A six-game trip was on tap, taking them to four of the "Original Six" cities, where the crowds would be hostile and intense. And the Knights would be playing without their star goaltender, as Marc-Andre Fleury was still on the shelf from the concussion he had sustained back on October 13, and there was no timetable for his return.

"With concussions, you can't predict," McPhee said after reporters asked when Fleury might be back in net. "But we're not going to rush Marc back."

Malcolm Subban's timetable was equally mystifying. He had a lower-body injury, not a concussion, but his return was also unknown. The reality was that neither goaltender was close to getting back on the ice, much less playing in an NHL game.

So that left it up to Oscar Dansk and Maxime Lagace, the two goalies who had begun the season in the minors, to backstop the Knights on the six-game road trip which would begin in Brooklyn on October 30 against the New York Islanders.

The Islanders were a befuddling team. There was talent, led by captain John Tavares, one of the game's elite players. There was Mathew Barzal, a promising rookie center who could skate fast and had unbelievable stick handling skills. He could play keep-away all by himself. They were complemented by a group of good, but not great players who worked hard and overachieved many nights.

The Islanders had plenty of flaws, however, not the least of which was the building they played in. The Barclays Center was not built for hockey and many of the seats had obstructed views. The Islanders had made a deal to move from the Nassau Coliseum, which had been their home since their inception in

1972, and the hope was the change in venue would grow their fan base.

But it was Year Three of that plan and it was evident the fans were not storming the doors to get in. The Isles were among the lowest teams in terms of home attendance, and while the building itself was modern and easy to access via public transit, it just didn't seem to be working.

Then there was the issue of the quality of the ice. The system the arena management chose to make the sheet wasn't the best and players from both home and visiting teams complained about it. Many players thought it was the worst in the league.

The Knights chose to stay in Manhattan for their trip as they were to face the New York Rangers the following night at Madison Square Garden, another building notorious for its bad ice. They chose to practice in New Jersey, skating at the New Jersey Devils' practice facility. So the team was getting a tour of the New York metropolitan area.

There was also a new face on the trip. Defenseman Shea Theodore had been recalled from the Chicago Wolves and veteran Jason Garrison had been assigned to the Wolves. Garrison was 32 years old; Theodore was 10 years his junior. He was a faster skater, had more upside offensively and fit in more with the big picture.

But coach Gerard Gallant decided to wait to insert Theodore in the lineup. He opted for Brad Hunt instead. Hunt had been signed as a free agent during the summer and had NHL experience with Edmonton, St. Louis and Nashville. And while that experience constituted just 33 games, he was a steady player who used his smarts. Although undersized at five feet, nine inches, Hunt was capable of handling himself physically against bigger forwards. He also was well-liked in the locker room. He never complained about ice time, accepted whatever role Gallant gave him, and when he got his chance, Hunt always gave his best effort.

With their record at 8-1, the hockey world began to take a more optimistic look at the Knights. Maybe these guys aren't so bad after all, some of the pundits were writing online and saying on the radio shows and podcasts. But all agreed that this would be a litmus test as to how good this team actually was.

Gallant didn't disagree.

"This is going to be a real test for us," he said. "We're going to play some very good teams in some tough buildings and we'll see what we're made of."

As the Knights left their locker room for the first game of the road trip, it was Dansk leading them onto the Barclays Center ice. He was off to a great start, having successfully held off the Blues, then beaten the Blackhawks and Avalanche. He had an NHL shutout as part of his ledger and his confidence was high.

"It's been great so far," Dansk said in realizing his dream. "The shooters in this league are very good, so you have to be alert. But the guys are playing great in front of me and making my job easy."

The Knights had a 2-1 lead as the second period was beginning to wind down, and while the Islanders had been creating chances, Dansk had repelled the majority of their attempts. But disaster was about to strike.

With James Neal in the penalty box for tripping, the Islanders pressed to pull even. Dansk looked to go from right to left across his crease to challenge the shooter. But he appeared to have caught his skate in a rut in the Barclays ice and he landed awkwardly. He was able get up but it was evident he was hurt. Moments later Tavares beat Dansk on the power play to tie the game 2-2.

Dansk flexed his left leg but he was unable to continue and he left the game with 5:10 to go in the period. Lagace was summoned off the bench and found himself the fourth goaltender to be used by the Knights in only 10 games. Like Dansk, his NHL experience consisted of part of one game in the preseason. Now he was in a 2-2 game in the regular season against an opponent which smelled blood in the water.

It was bizarre, to be sure. But there was no time to think about that. League was charged with keeping his team in the game and the Islanders didn't waste any time as Barzal scored to give the home team a 3-2 lead with 2:16 to go in the second. Lagace and the Knights survived the end of the period but the momentum had clearly shifted. Dansk had injured his left knee and would not return to the ice for a few months, much less the third period in Brooklyn. That left it to Lagace.

The Islanders were now in control. They scored three times in the first 12:38 to take a 6-2 lead and they cruised to a 6-3 victory, sending the 11,113 in attendance home happy.

But the Knights had a more pressing issue than having made history with their first road defeat. They were now playing a fourth-string goalie, and who would back him up? They were to play the Rangers the next night, and suddenly the option of having kept Calvin Pickard would not have looked so bad.

McPhee once again was faced with a hard decision — go out and trade for a goalie or stay with what he had and pray the team survived the trip. At worst, if the Knights lost all six games, they'd still have a winning record, and perhaps Fleury could be ready when the team returned home on November 10.

But he still needed a backup for Lagace. Back in September, McPhee had signed Dylan Ferguson, a former seventh-round pick of the Dallas Stars. The Knights had acquired Ferguson in a trade for defenseman Marc Methot.

Ferguson had been playing junior hockey for the Kamloops Blazers of the Western Hockey League, and he actually was the winning goaltender in the Knights' first-ever preseason game back on September 16 in Vancouver when he beat the Canucks 9-4. Now he was sitting in a restaurant in Kamloops, some 4,000 miles away, eating dinner when his cell phone rang. He had to get to New York immediately.

Ferguson left the restaurant, got his gear, packed a bag and headed to Vancouver for a red-eye flight to Toronto. From there he took a connecting flight to New York and made it to the team's hotel by early afternoon. Equipment manager Chris Davidson-Adams prepared a white road jersey with number 1 and Ferguson's nameplate while assigning him a spot in the cramped visitors locker room at Madison Square Garden.

This was the fourth iteration of the Garden, which was built in 1968 above Pennsylvania Station, a major railroad and transit hub in Manhattan. The Garden had undergone two major renovations after opening its doors, one in 1991 prior to the 1992 Democratic National Convention, where Bill Clinton was nominated to run for President, and the second in 2011. And while the Rangers enjoyed a modern, roomy locker room, the visitors were still banished to a small, cramped area to dress.

As the team bussed over to the Garden, not far from their lower Manhattan hotel, tragic events were unfolding. A man driving a truck plowed into pedestrians who were walking along the Hudson River, enjoying a fall afternoon and perhaps preparing for Halloween festivities later in the day. Eight people were killed, and 11 were injured in the incident that took place not far from the epicenter of the 9/11 attacks — the World Trade Center. The police called it an act of terrorism and referred to the perpetrator an Islamic extremist.

Ed Graney, the award-winning columnist for the Las Vegas Review-Journal who was on the trip to write about the Knights, had been talking to Assistant General Manager Kelly McCrimmon about the Knights' goaltending situation when he got a call from his office. Forget about hockey, he was told. Get down to lower Manhattan right away. Videographer Heidi Fang and Adam Hill, the paper's mixed martial arts reporter who was in town early for a UFC card that weekend, joined Graney as they navigated their way on the subway to cover the event.

The Knights, who had experience in dealing with tragedy stemming from October 1, now were in a role to support the Rangers. Several of the Rangers' players lived in the area where the attack took place. Goaltender Henrik Lundqvist, the team's most popular player, was worried for his family. After all, it was Halloween, the kids would be out trick-or-treating. Lundqvist was greatly relieved to learn his family was safe.

Still, a pall had fallen over the Garden. Unlike the Islanders, who were struggling to fill the Barclays Center on a consistent basis, the Rangers played to sellouts every night. Their fan base goes back generations to the old Garden on Eighth Avenue and West 50th Street, and their fans are among the most loyal in the entire NHL, despite having won just one Stanley Cup since

1940 and just four in the franchise's history, which dates back to 1926.

A moment of silence was observed for the attack victims, and the fans quickly tried to lift their team with the familiar "Let's Go Rangers!" chant. They didn't have to wait long as Jimmy Vesey, the former Harvard star who the Rangers had signed as a free agent the year before, beat Lagace just 2:45 into the match for a 1-0 lead.

But minutes later, Oscar Lindberg, who had played for the Rangers prior to being selected by the Knights in the expansion draft, tied the game for his fifth goal of the year after scoring just eight in 65 games with the Rangers the year before. Lindberg had been playing on the top line with Reilly Smith and Jonathan Marchessault and he appeared to be benefitting from it. He had just turned 26 two days before and he got a nice hand from the Garden fans.

Then, with 39 seconds left in the first period, Smith gave the Knights a 2-1 lead as he beat Lundqvist from in front after being set up by Marchessault. Lagace wasn't standing on his head in the Vegas net. But he was doing enough to keep his team in the game. The Knights were doing their part, using their speed to get into the New York zone and staying out of the penalty box.

After Mats Zuccarello tied it 2-2 at 1:29 of the second period, the Knights were able to retake the lead. Smith scored his second of the game 7:06 into the period to break the tie. Then with just over a minute to play in the period, David Perron was awarded a penalty shot after being hauled down from behind on a breakaway.

Perron, a crafty veteran, calmly collected the puck at center ice, picked up speed as he crossed the blue line, faked to his backhand to draw Lundqvist to that side, and used the opening to go back to his forehand and snap the puck through the small opening past the Rangers' goalie to make it 4-2.

The Knights were feeling good about themselves as the Zambonis cleaned the ice during the second intermission. Lagace was playing well enough. They had a two-goal lead. Maybe they could steal one and bounce back from the loss in Brooklyn.

Down the hall, the Rangers were regrouping. They were playing for their city as the events of lower Manhattan remained fresh in everyone's minds. They had renewed motivation. Surely they could solve some kid who was playing in just his second NHL game. No way were they going to let an expansion team come into their house and beat them.

Five and a half minutes in, with Perron in the penalty box serving the first of two tripping minors that had occurred on the same play, Chris Kreider cut it to 4-3. Less than four minutes later, it was 4-4 as Pavel Buchnevich beat Lagace.

The momentum had shifted, just as it had the night before. The Knights were being overwhelmed and when Colin Miller took a slashing penalty with 6:43 to play and Mika Zibanejad, the Rangers' talented center, scored to give his team a 5-4 lead, the visitors knew they were in big trouble.

Michael Grabner hit the empty net with 1:24 to go and the Rangers had come back to win 6-4. As they went to center ice and raised their sticks in salute to the 17,294 fans, the Knights trudged off the ice having made the wrong kind of history. It was the first time the team had lost consecutive games and they were now 0-2 on the road trip. Things weren't about to get any easier. The team was headed to Boston for a Thursday date with the Bruins.

"We sat back and let them take it to us in the third period," Gallant said. "That's two nights in a row we pissed away points. We've played four good periods here, and we have to play for 60 minutes."

Perron, whose penalty shot goal should have made him one of the heroes but whose tripping penalties gave the Rangers the opening they needed to get back in the game, took the blame. "I kind of let the team down on that one," Perron said. "Obviously, we talked before the game that we can't take many penalties to win on the road, and I was guilty of that tonight."

As for Lagace, his starting debut in the NHL didn't go the way he wanted, but he was philosophical about it.

"It's not the result we wanted, but I felt more comfortable," Lagace said. "I'm taking in the experience and having fun with all of that. I wish we won, but it's going to be — refocus for the next game."

The Bruins would be looking for revenge after having lost 3-1 on October 15. There was also some motivation among the Boston fans, thanks to a Twitter gaffe by the Golden Knights' social media team.

One of the big tasks in promoting sports in 2017 was the use of various platforms to get the message out on your team. Every pro team has its own staff that is charged with getting content to its website, using Twitter, Facebook, Instagram and other means to connect with its fan base.

The Knights embraced this from the beginning and even before they had hired McPhee as their general manager, they had hired Dan Marrazza to oversee their social media content.

Marrazza was from the East Coast and he knew the game. He also had a quick wit and just enough snark to make things fun. He sometimes ventured close to the line but never crossed it when it came to good taste.

But in the Knights' first meeting with the Bruins, Marrazza crossed it on Twitter. He introduced the Bruins' lineup using female names instead, playing off the 2012 movie "Ted". The majority of the team's followers didn't get the joke, which came across as misogynistic and simply downright stupid. Subsequent tweets during the game poked fun at the New England accent and were mildly funny at best.

McPhee was not amused. Neither was owner Bill Foley or president Kerry Bubolz. The Marrazza tweets came two weeks after the horrific shootings of October 1 and it undermined all the goodwill the team had built throughout the country.

The team issued a public apology, saying:

"Before Sunday's game against the Boston Bruins, we issued a series of tweets quoting a Boston-based movie with a bear as its main character that were in poor taste. By no means were the tweets intended to disparage females or female hockey players in any way. We do not condone sexism in any form and fully support the inclusive culture of hockey that makes our sport great. We accept full responsibility for our actions and apologize to those who were offended."

Marrazza was on the trip, and he was able to avoid the wrath of the Boston fans as he was safely ensconced in the press box at TD Garden. Not that anyone would recognize him anyway. He was an ordinary looking guy, tall, a bit gangly but he wasn't someone you could pick out in a crowd and yell, "Hey Dan!"

Dave Goucher was another story. He had been a fixture in Boston for decades, and as the Bruins' radio play-by-play announcer he had endeared himself to New England hockey fans going back to 2000. The Knights had hired him to be their television play-by-play voice as Goucher knew Eric Tosi, who had worked for the Bruins in media relations prior to joining the Knights in the summer of 2016 as VP of communications.

Goucher was paired with another former Bruin, Shane Hnidy, on the AT&T Sportsnet telecasts. Hnidy had played for the Bruins' 2011 Stanley Cup championship team and had been broadcasting games as an analyst since 2011, when he was working the Winnipeg Jets telecasts. He was sharp, funny, knew the game and had a good chemistry with Goucher, who was a pro's pro.

On the radio side, the Knights' games were being called by Dan D'Uva, a New jersey native who should not be confused with Dan Duva, the late boxing promoter from the Garden State. D'Uva had paid his dues doing minor league hockey in Trenton with the ECHL and the Syracuse Crunch of the AHL. He was solid, well-prepared, had a good voice and was quickly gaining popularity with the expansion team's fan base.

All three knew they shouldered a huge responsibility. People would hang on their every word and they not only had to make things entertaining, they had to be informative and educational. Remember, this was a market that was new to the sport, and while many knew the game, many more needed to learn about hockey. Goucher, Hnidy and D'Uva were going to be an important part of the learning process.

The Knights played the Bruins with more purpose and stayed out of the penalty box. They would take just one penalty — an interference call on Colin Miller in the second period. Miller was the player the Knights had selected from the Bruins in the expansion draft and he had been mobbed by the Boston media at the morning skate earlier in the day. He got the requisite "How does it feel to be back?" questions from the TV and radio reporters. The print guys, who had a deeper relationship with Miller, wanted to know how he was getting along living in Las Vegas and if he was surprised by the team's 8-3 start.

The game was 1-1 going into third period as Rick Nash's second-period goal was matched by Cody Eakin. But midway through the third period, Sean Kuraly broke the tie, beating Lagace and giving the Bruins a 2-1 lead. The Knights had a power play opportunity with 4:39 to play but were unable to beat Tuukka Rask, Boston's fine goaltender. Rask stopped 28 of the 29 shots he faced as the Bruins held on for the 2-1 victory, and the Knights' road trip continued its downward direction with a third straight loss.

Gallant was disappointed with the loss, but he had no problem with the effort. "I loved the way we competed," he said. "It was a good hockey game, well played by both sides. We had some chances but Rask was very good."

Perhaps almost as good was Lagace's play and the fact, for the second game in a row, the Knights' starting goaltender was still in the net at the end of play.

The Knights were headed to Canada and Ottawa, hoping to turn around the second half of the road trip. They would face the Senators, the Toronto Maple Leafs and the Montreal Canadiens in a four-day span before heading home. It was going to be a daunting challenge under the best of circumstances. But with a fourth-string goaltender in net, fatigue a likelihood and dealing with adversity for the first time as a franchise with a three-game losing streak, Gallant needed to do something to shake things up.

10. Change Is Coming

Late in the game against the Boston Bruins, Gerard Gallant had moved William Karlsson up to the first line with Reilly Smith and Jonathan Marchessault. Gallant had coached Smith and Marchessault when he was the Florida Panthers' coach and he knew them well.

But Karlsson was someone he was still learning about. He liked the center's "200-foot game", which saw Karlsson tend to his defensive responsibilities and not focus solely on scoring goals. He was also proving to be a good penalty killer, a role he had developed while in Columbus.

Oscar Lindberg had a great October. He had five goals and appeared on his way to a career season. He had done nothing wrong. But sometimes you have to make change for change's sake, so Gallant replaced one Swede in Lindberg for another Swede, Karlsson, to center the Golden Knights' top line.

Karlsson had a quicker release than Lindberg. He was a faster skater, stronger and exceptionally bright. He, along with James Neal, were arguably the team's smartest players when it came to hockey IQ He always seemed to be in the right place at the right time to make a play.

But that wasn't Gallant's only move. He promoted center Erik Haula to the second line, skating with Neal and David

Perron. Cody Eakin, who had played in the middle on that line the first month, and played well, was dropped down to the third line where he would skate with Alex Tuch and either Lindberg or Brendan Leipsic.

The fourth line, consisting of Pierre-Edouard Bellemare centering for Tomas Nosek and Will Carrier, stayed intact. Gallant loved the tenacity of the Bellemare line, the way they forechecked and kept the momentum going for the next line's shift. Bellemare and Nosek were also proving to be adept penalty killers, and Gallant liked to keep his penalty-killing forward pairs together so as to not disrupt the continuity of the lines once the Knights killed a penalty or were scored upon.

His penalty killers would be Karlsson and Smith, Eakin and Leipsic, or Lindberg and Bellemare and Nosek. He could also use Haula and Perron if needed.

Gallant had no idea if the moves of shifting his centers around would work. No coach can ever predict what the outcome of making changes will yield. He was merely hoping for something good to happen right away, to get his team out of its early tailspin.

"You hope for the best," Gallant said of the moves. "If it doesn't work, you try something else."

Right away, there appeared to be good chemistry with both moves. Karlsson fit right in with Smith and Marchessault, and they quickly got comfortable with one another on the ice. They were unselfish and fast, and their skill-sets seemed to compliment each other.

Smith was blue collar, working the corners, taking hits to keep the play alive, while Marchessault was a true sniper, willing to throw the puck at the goal at every opportunity, understanding that hockey is the kind of game where you never know what might happen once you send that round piece of vulcanized rubber toward the net.

Karlsson was also strong on the puck and he had that quick release. He also had a great sense of timing, being able to shoot the puck as it was sent his way, one-timing it as players say, and doing it with deadly accuracy.

Haula had been trying to keep his job in the Minnesota Wild organization, and he was not George McPhee's intended target as the NHL expansion draft drew close. McPhee had his sights set on Matt Dumba, the Wild's talented young defenseman who McPhee thought would be a great fit on the Vegas blue line.

But the Wild didn't want to lose Dumba. Chuck Fletcher, then Minnesota's GM, asked McPhee to consider a deal which would enable the Wild to keep Dumba. He would consider such a deal, but it would come at a high price. McPhee would pass on Dumba and would take Haula, who was originally from Finland and who had been a star at the University of Minnesota before the hometown Wild drafted him in the seventh round in 2009.

Haula was fast and good with the puck, and he would no doubt be motivated, having been a fourth-line player and a healthy scratch playing for Bruce Boudreau the year before. In addition, the Wild would send Alex Tuch to Vegas for a third-round draft pick.

It would be a couple of moves that Fletcher would regret, and it contributed to his ultimate demise as the Wild's general manager.

Like Karlsson, Haula was playing with a couple of veterans in Neal and Perron and their games were very divergent. Neal was a power forward who set up in front and worked the corners. He also had been to the Stanley Cup Final the year before with Nashville and had played with Fleury on the Pittsburgh Penguins. And while Neal's name wasn't on the Stanley Cup, he knew how to win and he was highly motivated every night he stepped onto the ice.

Perron had bounced around from team to team. The Golden Knights were his fifth different NHL team in six years. He had played twice in St. Louis but also played in Edmonton, Pittsburgh and Anaheim. But he was a heady player, one who could hang on to the puck and draw additional defenders to him, leaving teammates open.

Perron was also a skilled passer and he played with a bit of an edge that opposing players didn't care for. He could get under your skin.

Together, they seemed to connect early on. Haula used his speed to elude defenders, and Neal and Perron knew what spots to get to. And they found themselves getting quality scoring opportunities.

The hockey world was embracing analytics and the Knights were no exception. Mathematical systems and probabilities were being churned out to determine a team's strengths and deficiencies, and the Knights' man in that department was Misha Donskov. He had worked with McPhee for Team Canada, had coached in junior hockey prior to that and had NHL front office experience with the Columbus Blue Jackets and the Atlanta Thrashers. But unlike Corsi and Fenwick, two of the most popular analytic systems, Donskov developed his own system and had success with it.

McPhee said of analytics when he was hired: "It's not the be-all, end-all, but it is part of the game and anything we can use to help our team be successful, we will embrace it. It's part of what we do but not all that we do."

Gallant essentially lost his job in Florida because he didn't totally buy into the analytical bend the Panthers had taken in building their team and the way now-General Manager Tom Rowe wanted him to coach it. Gallant was old-school hockey and he coached by feel, not by a spread sheet. He trusted his eyes and his gut, and his gut was telling him to play William Karlsson on the first line and Erik Haula on the second line.

The Ottawa Senators had been to the Eastern Conference Finals the year before, and led by their all-world defenseman Erik Karlsson, they were expected to challenge for the Stanley Cup. Karlsson had played in the 2017 postseason with a mangled ankle which would require surgery in the off-season. But after missing all of the 2018 preseason and the first five games of the regular season, he was back on the blue line and giving the Senators a huge boost. Ottawa actually had a winning record going into the visit from the Knights, and the Sens, as their fan base called them, were 6-2-5. Their first three games went to shootouts and they were involved in five shootouts during the first month of the season.

But things weren't all that rosy in the suburb of Kanata, where the Senators played their home games. The fans, who had stayed away during the playoff run, continued to avoid the Canadian Tire Centre as if it was infested with bedbugs. Ottawa was closer to the bottom of the league in attendance that it was to the top. Sections of the 18,572-seat arena's upper deck were draped in banners to give the illusion the joint wasn't the ghost town everyone knew it to be.

Owner Eugene Melnyk was trying to get a new arena built in downtown Ottawa. But there was little appetite to use public funding on an arena. Meanwhile, Erik Karlsson was balking at signing a contract extension and was looking to test the free agent waters when he would become an unrestricted free agent in 2019. In addition, there was growing speculation the Senators were about to make a major trade with Colorado and obtain disenchanted center Matt Duchene and maybe move Kyle Turris, one of the team's more popular players.

So there was no shortage of distractions when the Saturday matinee got underway. The Knights rolled out their revamped lineup and struck first as Tuch scored a power-play goal 4:25 in. But the Senators answered 21 seconds into the second period as Mark Stone tied it. Suddenly, it became a wide-open, back-and-forth shootout with the teams trading goals. Haula and Marchessault scored for Vegas, Alex Burrows for Ottawa. After 40 minutes, the Knights had a 3-2 lead.

Twice before on the trip, they had squandered leads. Would this be the same scenario? William Karlsson and Haula saw that the script would be different as they scored three minutes and eighteen seconds apart to give the Knights a 5-2 lead.

The Senators got as close as 5-4 as Erik Karlsson scored his first of the year with 34 seconds to play after goaltender Craig Anderson had been pulled for a sixth attacker. But the Knights and Lagace held on, leaving Canada's capital with a hard-fought but well-deserved 5-4 win while snapping their losing streak at three games.

"As a team, we felt we got a lot better in Boston, and we wanted that to continue that Saturday," said Haula. "It wasn't easy, but that's how it goes, that's how you end streaks like that."

Gallant said: "It was a real strong game. They made it close at the end, but we got the two points, and I liked the way the team played for the most part. We were able to dump it in and get behind their defense, and it was a good job executing the game plan. I thought we played well from the start, and I definitely think there was some carry-over from Thursday in Boston to Saturday."

Lagace's parents were among the 16,284 in attendance to see him get his first NHL win. "It was a really good team effort, and it's good for the road trip to get a win and break the losing streak," Lagace said. "I'm learning with each game, and I'm getting more comfortable playing with the guys in front of me."

The mood was upbeat as the team made the short flight to Toronto for Monday's game with the Maple Leafs. Toronto is the nexus of the hockey universe and the Leafs enjoy a national fan base across Canada. Tickets to games at the Air Canada Centre are expensive and scarce. There has been talk from time to time of putting a second NHL team in Toronto because of the amount of interest in the sport emanating from the city.

Unlike Las Vegas, where the players could walk down the Strip incognito, such a luxury does not exist in Toronto. A Knights player wouldn't last more than a few steps outside the hotel without being recognized and likely besieged by autograph and selfie seekers. But it's also the kind of atmosphere that players crave to compete in.

The Leafs last won the Stanley Cup in 1967. The drought was now into the next half-century, and the fans were cautiously optimistic that the franchise was on a path to end the drought. Auston Matthews, the talented center who was the rookie of the year in 2017, was the linchpin of the team. Matthews, an American who grew up in Arizona and had played in a youth hockey tournament in Las Vegas when he was 15 years old, was shouldering an immense burden. Unlike other star athletes with Toronto's other pro sports teams, the baseball Blue Jays and the NBA Raptors, Matthews was subjected to far greater scrutiny.

So when the Leafs held their morning skate and Matthews exited after just six minutes with some apparent circulation issues in his leg, Toronto held its collective breath. The news broke quickly on social media, and coach Mike Babcock only added to the speculation when he said very little about Matthews' availability, stating only that his star's presence would be a game-time decision.

The afternoon sports talk shows were dealing with the news as freaked-out callers worried their team would be without their star for a long stretch and the show hosts tried to talk callers off the ledge while debating among themselves exactly how long might Matthews be out and what the ramifications could be?

Well guess what? The pregame warmups got underway and Number 34, Matthews, was on the ice. He would play 29 shifts, skate for 21:11 and assist on James van Riemsdyk's first-period goal which put Toronto ahead 2-1 after Nazem Kadri and James Neal had exchanged goals 38 seconds apart.

Trailing 3-1 in the second period, the Knights' resiliency came to the fore. First it was Reilly Smith, a Toronto native, cutting it to 3-2 with 1:10 to go before intermission. Then Deryk Engelland scored 6:16 into the third to tie it 3-3 as he beat Frederik Andersen from the top of the right face-off circle.

After a thrilling five-minute overtime that saw both teams have great chances to win it, the Knights were involved in their first-ever shootout. The shootout is a series of penalty shot opportunities — the skater against the goalie. It's a best-of-three scenario and then goes to sudden death if necessary. Hockey purists loathe it, but among mainstream fans it has become an acceptable if not exciting way to determine a winner. Besides, the Knights we're guaranteed a point in the standings no matter what happened, thanks to the game going into overtime. So now they were essentially playing for the second point.

The Leafs opted to go first and Mitch Marner beat Lagace for a 1-0 lead. The Knights used Smith, and Andersen stopped his attempt. Lagace then stopped Matthews, and Andersen denied Neal. After Lagace was able to stop Patrick Marleau, that left it up to Perron. He had scored on a penalty shot against the Rangers less than a week ago, but this was different. If he scores, the Knights remain alive and the shootout continues. He skated in, tried to deke Andersen out of position but wound up missing the net. The Leafs won 4-3 and the Knights were now 1-3-1 on the trip, which was to conclude the next night in Montreal.

If hockey is the center of the universe in Toronto, it is religion in Montreal. The Canadiens are the standard by which everyone else is measured. Their 24 Stanley Cup championships are nearly double that of any other NHL franchise. The Maple Leafs are next with 13 Cups.

The Canadiens play in the 21,288-seat Bell Centre, the largest building in the league in terms of seating capacity. Every game is sold out, and the Canadiens are one of the few things the Anglo- and French-Canadians can agree on in the multi-lingual city of Montreal.

For Perron and Marchessault, it was a homecoming of sorts. Both grew up in Quebec, and the local media, particularly the French-speaking, wanted to talk to them. Fleury obviously was not with the team, but he would have been the main target of the Montreal press.

Both players appeared comfortable conversing with the French-speaking media and everyone was hoping to come away with a point and head home to Las Vegas on an up note.

The Canadiens needed the points as much, if not more.They had gotten off to a horrific 2-8 start. The fans were calling for Coach Michel Therrien's head and that of General Manager Marc Bergevin. What's worse, Carey Price, the team's franchise goaltender, was injured and no one knew when he would return. So when they dropped the puck, the goaltenders were Maxime Lagace for Vegas and Charlie Lindgren for Montreal.

Lindgren had just three games of NHL experience when he was called up from the Canadiens' AHL farm team in Laval, Quebec, so it was difficult to guess what would happen.

Montreal jumped out to a 2-0 lead midway through the first period on goals from Brendan Gallagher and Jordie Benn, the brother of Dallas Stars star forward Jamie Benn. Bellemare got one of the goals back late in the first period and it was 2-1 going into the second period.

But Max Pacioretty beat Lagace to give the Habs a 3-1 lead while Lindgren was playing amazing hockey in the Montreal net. He would face 31 shots and stopped all but two of them, the last coming from Marchessault with 1:37 to play, which cut it to 3-2. And that's the way it ended, with the Canadiens getting a much-needed win and the Knights ending their trip on a down note. They didn't play badly, but it was far from the result they were seeking.

Of a possible 12 points on the six-game road trip, the Knights managed to secure just three. They were 1-4-1 and heading home with a 9-5-1 record.

"I think you look at the positives and try to build on those," said defenseman Brad Hunt. "Sure, we would have liked to have picked up a few more points. But we played fairly well, and I think we learned a lot about each other. It was a good bonding experience."

The Golden Knights' fans last saw their team on October 27. It was now November 10 and although it was going to be a brief visit, the Knights were glad to reunite with their fans.

By now the fans had gotten to know Lagace, the current starting goaltender. They liked Lagace well enough, but they missed Marc-Andre Fleury. Unfortunately, Fleury was still working his way through recuperation from the concussion he sustained back on October 13, so they weren't going to see him for a while.

Coach Gerard Gallant was pleased with the moves he had made on the road trip, and he was keeping William Karlsson with Reilly Smith and Jonathan Marchessault, and Erik Haula remained the center on the second line with James Neal and David Perron.

The Winnipeg Jets were visiting T-Mobile Arena. By now, two trends had been established. One, the visiting team's fans were making the excursion to Las Vegas to watch their team. Two, the visiting team was having a tough time winning in T-Mobile Arena.

Some believed the opposing team was suffering from a bout of "Vegas Flu". The theory was that visiting teams would be out partying all night and not have much energy to play. It was an interesting theory, but it was just that — a theory.

Virtually every team kept close to their hotel and the players preferred to have dinner via room service or would go out as a group. Very few ventured out to the Strip or took in a show while in town.

As for where the visiting teams stayed, it varied. Some stayed on the Las Vegas Strip close to T-Mobile Arena, where players could walk to the rink. Others opted to stay away from the Strip, though the options were fewer.

There are hotels in Las Vegas that don't have casinos, but that didn't seem to be an issue. The bigger issue was making sure all players stayed out of the sports books. The league had security personnel in town and reminded teams when they arrived that visiting a sports book or placing a bet on an NHL game was strictly verboten.

But if a player wanted to play a few hands of blackjack, there was nothing anyone could do to stop him, provided, of course, he was 21 years of age or older.

So while the "Vegas Flu" notion was amusing and some tried to sell it as legitimate, the truth was the Golden Knights were a good hockey team who had a strong fan base and enjoyed a real home-ice advantage.

At least that was the case most nights. When the Jets came out of their locker room for the pregame warmups, they were greeted by a couple thousand of their fans who had made the trip from Winnipeg. A few Winnipeg residents had even bought Golden Knights season tickets to guarantee they had tickets for this game. They would sell off the other games to try and make back the money they had invested.

On this night, the Jets' fans would leave disappointed. The Knights never trailed, holding leads of 2-0, 3-1, 3-2 and eventually pulling away for a 5-2 win. William Karlsson scored twice, giving him six goals in 14 games. His season-best had been nine goals two years before with Columbus. Assuming he stayed healthy, which on this team was proving to be no sure thing, Karlsson would easily eclipse that mark, perhaps before Thanksgiving.

But just as soon as the Knights were home, they were back on the road, returning to Canada. The Edmonton Oilers had one of the game's best players in center Connor McDavid. He could do it all and he was the person the Oilers' fan base pinned its hopes on to return the franchise to the glory days of the mid-to-late 1980s, when Wayne Gretzky, Mark Messier and Co. were winning five Stanley Cups.

However, Edmonton got off to a slow start. The Oilers were struggling at 6-9-2, and the natives were getting restless at Rogers Place, the team's beautiful 18,550-seat arena that was the anchor of a massive downtown redevelopment project called the "Ice District." Forget winning a sixth Cup. The fans were hoping their team could find its way and just make the playoffs.

For one night, the Oilers looked like a playoff team. They jumped all over the Knights, building a 4-0 lead early in the second period before Pierre-Edouard Bellemare temporarily stopped the bleeding. But McDavid was dominant and he scored twice. Ryan Nugent-Hopkins also had a pair of goals as the Oilers chased Lagace from the net in the third period, and Gallant gave Dylan Ferguson his first taste of the NHL in the regular season. Ferguson played the final 9:14 and made a nifty save on McDavid, which got him a stick tap on the pads from the Edmonton captain and a cool story he could tell his kids and grandkids years from now.

The Oilers left the ice 8-2 winners and the Knights once again had to quickly turn the page. They were scheduled to be in Vancouver two nights later and Gallant expected a much better effort.

He got it as the Knights jumped out to a 2-0 lead behind goals from Perron and Karlsson. But the Canucks, who were being led by first-year Coach Travis Green, rallied behind their rookie star, Brock Boeser, and Bo Horvat to tie it 2-2 late in the second period.

The Knights had shown an ability to be resilient and that trait came through in the final 20 minutes. They tightened things up in their own end. Lagace, who was back in the net as the starter, was strong, and Haula would deliver the game-winner by beating Jacob Markstrom 6:27 into the period. Marchessault and Smith capped the scoring as the Knights left Vancouver with a 5-2 win and a split of the quick two-game road trip.

A look at the Pacific Division standings on November 17 saw the Knights in second place with 23 points, one behind Los Angeles. The expansion upstarts weren't fading into oblivion like everyone thought. Instead, people we're starting to sing their praises as a team that played hard every night, could skate and forecheck, and somehow was managing to win despite playing a fourth-string goaltender.

Now the schedule called for four division games in a row, beginning with a home game against the Kings November 19. This was one of the most anticipated dates on the calendar, and not just because it was LA and the Kings' fans who would be invading the Strip in droves.

It was a chance to take over the top spot in the division, make a statement to the Kings and everyone else in the division that the Knights would be in this thing for the foreseeable future, perhaps all the way into the first week of April.

For the first time there were interesting discussions on the various hockey websites that had tried to be part of the Golden Knights' experience. They were floating the idea that maybe this team was good enough to make the playoffs. Never mind that it wasn't even Thanksgiving and the season was just 18 games old. To Gallant and his players this was the kind of poisonous talk they didn't want to hear, nor did they need to respond to.

"We're just taking it one game at a time," Gallant told reporters. It would become a familiar mantra, one he would repeat over and over so often that those who covered the team on a daily basis stopped taking notes because they knew what was coming.

So with a chance to move into first place in the division, the Knights and Kings squared off on a Sunday afternoon at T-Mobile Arena. As expected, the game drew a huge throng of LA fans, and while the talk of playoff hockey was abetted in the locker room, it felt like a playoff atmosphere.

Before every game, the Knights player who was facing his former team would be asked what his emotions were going to be like, and did he hold any grudges against his previous employers? The responses were virtually identical — "I was with a great group of guys and now I'm with another great group of guys", or "I was just looking for an opportunity and I'm trying to take advantage of it", or "I didn't know what to expect when Vegas selected me but so far it's been great."

In other words, nobody was rocking the boat. The one player who had trouble adjusting was no longer with the team. Vadim Shipachyov had run out of chances after he was once again returned to the AHL, and this time, he was suspended without pay after he refused to report in late October.

Shipachyov played just three games with the Knights, scored one goal and couldn't crack the lineup. General manager George McPhee knew he had to cut ties with the disgruntled Russian center who basically wanted to go home. But he was under contract to the Knights and nobody was willing to trade for Shipachyov and his $9 million deal.

With things in limbo and a potential cancer festering, the league got involved. If Shipachyov wanted out, he could retire from the NHL. His contract would be voided and the Knights would keep most of the $9 million, including the $2 million signing bonus they paid the player. Vegas would retain Shipachyov's NHL rights for the next five years though it would be unlikely he would want to come back. If he waited out the five years, he would be near 36 years old and the likelihood of another NHL team signing him seemed remote.

On November 9, the deal was done. Shiapachyov was headed back to the KHL to play for his old team, SKA St. Petersburg, and the Knights had rid themselves of a possible problem in their locker room.

"Sometimes things just don't work out," McPhee said in what was the understatement of the year. In many respects, McPhee came out of it fairly clean. Shipachyov got some money but the bulk of it remained with the Golden Knights. And while Shipachyov ripped the team upon his return to Russia, McPhee wasn't losing any sleep over it. His team was playing good hockey and challenging for first place in its division.

As the game with the Kings got underway, the Knights came out with something to prove. Karlsson scored twice as part of a three-goal barrage in the first 11:22 and chased Kings goaltender Jonathan Quick in the process. Darcy Kuemper took over and his team rallied in front of him, cutting the deficit to 3-2 midway through the third period. But Alex Tuch sealed the 4-2 win with an empty-net goal with 1:02 to play.

The Knights had 25 points and were right on the Kings' heels. Brayden McNabb, the Kings player taken by the Knights in the expansion draft, had a big game, finishing with four hits, including one where he rocked former teammate Drew Doughty with a heavy hit into the boards near center ice.

Doughty wasn't impressed with the Knights' performance, saying that when all was said and done it would be the Kings with the better record. Those were words that would be remembered by the Knights' players, and it helped plant the seeds of a rivalry.

Another rivalry looking to sprout roots was with the Anaheim Ducks. The first meeting was slated for Thanksgiving Eve at the Honda Center in Anaheim. The Ducks had done some historic things themselves in their first year in the NHL, posting 33 wins, same as the Florida Panthers who had entered the league the same year. They had a Stanley Cup championship to their credit in 2007 and they had an enthusiastic fan base in Orange County.

They hated the Kings. They disliked the San Jose Sharks. Now, they had one more team to loathe.

And when the Ducks jumped out to a 2-0 lead, their fans were expecting a big win and a happy Thanksgiving. Their roster had been crippled by injuries to Ryan Kesler and Ryan Getzlaf. But they still had a star in goaltender John Gibson who was more than capable of winning games on his own. Now, staked to a two-goal lead, it seemed like a daunting task for the visitors.

But Marchessault scored on a power play late in the second period to cut it to 2-1. Colin Miller tied it 2:21 into the third period and James Neal tallied the game-winner at the 11:18 mark. Karlsson hit the empty net with two minutes to go to close out the scoring in a 4-2 Golden Knights win. For Karlsson, it was a night to celebrate as he scored his 10th goal of the year, eclipsing his career-best of nine with the Blue Jackets.

More important, the Vegas Golden Knights were going to celebrate Thanksgiving in first place in the Pacific Division. They were 13-6-1 with 27 points, one ahead of the second-place Kings.

"It's a big win tonight," Gallant said. "I thought our team played excellent all night long, and somebody said we are in first place. Is that official? Perfect."

Perfect indeed. Now, could they stay at the top of the division?

The night after celebrating Thanksgiving in Las Vegas with family and friends, the Knights hosted the San Jose Sharks, a very good team which two years ago had made it to the Stanley Cup Final only to lose to Fleury and the Pittsburgh Penguins.

The Sharks had a superstar in defenseman Brent Burns who had an unkept scraggly beard and a gap-toothed smile. Burns looked like he could be a professional wrestler. They also had veteran centers Joe Thornton and Joe Pavelski who were capable of doing damage offensively. And they had a smart, sharp coach in Peter DeBoer who was well-respected in the hockey world.

But the Knights weren't impressed. They jumped on the Sharks early as Shea Theodore scored 2:33 in, then James Neal made it 2-0 with his 12th goal of the year at the 11:16 mark. The Sharks got one back late in the first period but the Knights dominated in period two, with Karlsson scoring twice in a 6:55 span to make it 4-1 and chasing Martin Jones from the net.

But the Knights had shown a propensity for letting teams back into games. Sure enough, here came San Jose, riding goals from Burns, Chris Tierney and Mikkel Boedker to tie the game 4-4 and send it to overtime. The Sharks had all the momentum. But Marchessault short-circuited that momentum by winning it 1:21 into OT. The Knights' resiliency had once again saved them.

"We should have never let them come back, but that's our group, the way we're built, and we came back and got the two points," Marchessault said. "That's the only thing we're looking at right now."

The team had also welcomed back Malcolm Subban to the lineup as he took Lagace's spot early in the third period. It was his first action since getting hurt against St. Louis October 21.

The next night it was back to Arizona for a third meeting with the Coyotes. Rick Tocchet had replaced Dave Tippett as the team's coach and the hope was he could get things moving in the right direction. But a horrendous start saw the Desert Dogs holding the worst record in the entire NHL. And while the team was playing a little better, there was little hope of staging a major turnaround.

There would be no progress on this night. While on a second-period penalty kill, Tomas Nosek got things going by picking the pocket of Oliver Ekman-Larsson, the Coyotes' star defenseman, then beating Marek Langhamer, who was in the Arizona net. Thirty-one seconds later, Karlsson made it 2-0 as he one-timed Marchessault's pass past Langhamer. It was

Karlsson's 13th of the season and he certainly was taking full advantage of his opportunity to play on the top line.

Haula then scored on a power play 1:11 later to make it 3-0, and for the second straight game the Knights had chased the opposing team's starting goalie. Scott Wedgwood mopped up, and despite the Coyotes cutting the deficit to 3-2 they could not pull even as Marchessault scored into the empty net with two seconds left. The Knights left Gila River Arena with a 4-2 win.

Subban got the start and stopped 23 of the 25 shots he faced. He appeared to be fine physically. It was a sign of some normalcy returning to the roster, and Lagace had done a credible job filling in.

But while Subban was back, the Knights were losing someone else. This time, it was Will Carrier, the rugged forward who played just 7:23 after sustaining an upper-body injury against Arizona. He would not return until early January.

Still, there was optimism throughout the visitors' locker room. The Golden Knights were still in first place with a 15-6-1 record and 31 points. More important, they were finding ways to win and they were displaying enough quality depth that could sustain them through injuries or poor play. Gallant wasn't afraid to make changes and sit someone who wasn't getting results.

He also knew that success can be fleeting. Just as quickly as you enjoy it, it can disappear.

11. Fathers Know Best

Sometimes a little fatherly advice and support can come in handy. The Golden Knights were in need of a collective hug after having finished November and beginning December with three straight losses, including the franchise's first shutout, a 3-0 defeat to Dallas at T-Mobile Arena on November 28. Back-to-back road losses to Minnesota (4-2) and Winnipeg (7-4) had the team in another three-game losing streak.

They had also dropped out of first place in the Pacific Division and not only trailed the Los Angeles Kings by four points, they were only a point ahead of third-place San Jose and Vancouver, which had suddenly caught fire and was playing good hockey. Two points back was Calgary and two points behind the Flames was Anaheim. A couple more losses and the Knights would be headed towards the bottom of the division.

Once the NHL schedule had come out, plans were developed to have the players' fathers join the team for a road trip. They would also take in a home game from a suite at T-Mobile Arena. Katy Boettinger, the team's director of hockey administration, and Rick Braunstein, the director of travel services, would oversee the trip and the myriad details.

This was no simple feat. Remember, all the players' families lived outside of Las Vegas, so it meant arranging air transportation, lodging and ground transportation for the dads. Some were coming from as far away as Sweden and Finland.

But Boettinger and Braunstein are very good at what they do. They made the necessary arrangements well in advance, and early on December 3 the first dads arrived to watch their sons play Arizona. The Knights had owned the Coyotes so far, and this was their fourth meeting. The Coyotes were also the perfect antidote for a losing streak.

It was a back-and-forth affair, with the Coyotes answering each time they fell behind. This one went to overtime and Reilly Smith would be the hero, scoring with 1:10 remaining as Jonathan Marchessault set him up perfectly and Smith beat Scott Wedgewood.

Two days later, just about all the dads were in Las Vegas and they watched their boys beat Anaheim 4-3 in a shootout. Alex Tuch got the game-winner, which was only fitting as he had been robbed in the first period by a sensational glove save by John Gibson. The Knights had put the brakes on the losing streak, and as they boarded their flight to Nashville for the "Dads Trip", they did so having won two straight.

The tradition reportedly began when the Buffalo Sabres would allow a couple of dads to tag along on a road trip. But the Nashville Predators like to claim that they began including all the dads back in 1999, when Barry Trotz was their coach and he thought it would help foster team bonding.

It proved popular, and just about every NHL team does it. Some include the players' mothers, and they do a "Moms only trip".

For the Knights' trip, the stops would be Nashville and Dallas, ironically two tourist towns where the dads could have some fun while their sons went to work and would also be able to enjoy the games in the comfort of a luxury suite.

To no one's surprise, Las Vegas became a popular choice for opposing teams to take their dads and moms. And the Knights were equally accommodating, making sure the visiting team's parents were looked after and treated in a first-class manner with their own suite, completely catered and segregated from any potential trouble caused by over-zealous Knights fans.

For one dad in particular, this trip was going to be somewhat awkward. Karl Subban had a son who played for the Predators, all-star defenseman P.K., and another son, Malcolm, who would start in goal for the Golden Knights.

But dad didn't see it that way. He was going to enjoy the moment.

"It's probably not so much that I'll be cheering for Nashville or rooting for Vegas, but I'm just going to try and enjoy it," he said. "It's like being at your child's graduation, but tonight I'll have two kids walking across the stage. I'll be filled with joy. But I'm going to be very nervous. Hopefully, they're not going to lose any sleep over it and we'll have a good game.

"Usually, whenever I am in Nashville, I have the Nashville colors on, but today I'll probably be very neutral," he said. "I don't want Malcolm to look up and see me wearing something I shouldn't be wearing. I just want to be there and enjoy the game, and the best team will win."

The Knights staked Malcolm Subban to a 2-0 lead in the second period and things were going well for Karl's kid the goalie. But the Predators came roaring back and took a 3-2 lead with just over five minutes to play. And while P.K. Subban had failed to register a point in any of the three Nashville goals, Karl had gotten his wish. It was a good game and both teams would pick up a point as it went to overtime after Erik Haula tied it 3-3 with 40 seconds remaining.

The game ultimately went to a shootout, with Reilly Smith scoring the winner in the sixth round and Malcolm Subban slamming the door on his brother and the Predators by stopping all six shooters he faced. He had already made a career-high 41 stops prior to the shootout, and he was mobbed by his teammates while brother P.K. left the ice.

"It was something special, obviously, with all of my family watching back home, having my dad here, and beating my brother," Malcolm Subban said. "It was an unbelievable experience."

There was a joyous mood as the team boarded its charter flight to Dallas. Fathers and sons celebrated, commiserated and had a chance to catch up with each other. The players routinely called or texted their families during the season, but it was rare for them to have time for face-to-face conversations and talk about how mom was doing, or what was the latest with siblings and friends. It was what made the trip special.

The Stars were laying in wait as the teams prepared to meet for the third time. Ben Bishop, Dallas' all-star goaltender, was healthy and playing well. Jamie Benn, the team's leading scorer, was starting to find the net with more regularity.

Maxime Lagace was in net for Vegas and he knew he had to be sharp. He would face 15 first-period shots as the teams traded goals, and it was 1-1 heading into the second period. It was 2-2 with 5:25 gone in the middle frame when Smith and Brayden McNabb scored within a 2:25 span to give the Knights a 4-2 lead. Cody Eakin, the player the Knights had selected from Dallas during the expansion draft, assisted on McNabb's goal.

Benn cut it to 4-3 at 4:16 into the third and the Stars kept pushing for the equalizer. But Lagace and his defense continued to thwart Dallas, and Haula sealed the win by hitting the empty net with 43 seconds remaining.

For Haula, it was his 11th goal of the season, just four shy of his career best, and the season was just a third of the way complete. He had found a home centering for Perron and Neal, and the Knights had two high-octane scoring lines, a great fourth line that could check and shut down the opposition, and a third line that could do a little of everything.

They were still in second place in their division, trailing Los Angeles by four points. And with 19 wins and plenty of hockey left to be played, there was talk that the Knights could eclipse the record for wins by an expansion team, which was 33.

But the best news of all was the team was about to get its franchise player back.

Marc-Andre Fleury had been out of public view for the last six weeks after suffering a concussion back on October 13. Somehow, the Golden Knights managed to overcome having their star goaltender out of the lineup, as they were 19-10-1 heading into an important five-game homestead that would take them to Christmas and possibly define them for the remainder of their inaugural season.

Fleury had seen a couple of neurologists, and on their advice he stayed off the ice until he was 100 percent healthy. He was able to work out on his own, lift weights and run on the treadmill so his conditioning didn't suffer much. Fleury always kept himself in great shape and he had amazing flexibility for a 32-year-old athlete. It allowed him to make the acrobatic saves he was famous for.

On December 6, he practiced with the team, a big moment in his plan to return to action. He had no problems, and he was looking forward to playing again.

"It was great being back on the ice with my teammates for a full practice today," Fleury said in a text message released by the team. He was not made available for interviews after practice. "I am hopeful I can join the team for game action soon. We have been playing well and I am looking forward to getting back and doing what I can to help the team win."

Gallant said Fleury's return provided an emotional boost. "The guys were excited to see him out there," he said. "To get him back out there with the boys, there's nothing better than that."

Fleury's agent Allan Walsh has been a harsh critic of the NHL, and particularly of commissioner Gary Bettman when it came to concussions and head injuries. Many former players complained of cognitive issues in their post-hockey lives, but the league seemed to be in denial about the sensitive, yet important issue.

Walsh stopped short of criticizing the Golden Knights for allowing Fleury to continue playing after his collision with Anthony Mantha in the second period of the October 13 game with Detroit. The protocols being what they were, Fleury had been cleared and he wanted to continue. But in the aftermath of the injury, he second-guessed himself and said it probably wasn't a good idea to keep playing.

But he was now ready to return, and on December 12 he was in the starting lineup as the five-game homestand kicked off against the Carolina Hurricanes.

And while everyone was glad to see Fleury back after he had missed 25 games, all eyes were focused on the next game in two days. The Pittsburgh Penguins, Fleury's former team, would be coming to T-Mobile Arena, and it was one of two dates everyone circled when the schedule had been released back in June. The other date? February 6 in Pittsburgh.

A media crush was expected for the Penguins game. On most nights the press box at T-Mobile had dozens of empty seats. But with Sidney Crosby & Company due to arrive, space was filling up fast. Not only was this a big story in Las Vegas and Pittsburgh, it was a big national story for those who covered hockey.

Fleury was already being asked about facing the Penguins, the team he helped win three Stanley Cups with after they selected him No. 1 overall in the 2003 draft. He politely steered the conversation away, saying the team had a game before that and his focus was on Carolina.

It was the correct answer. A big part of the team's mindset had always been to never look beyond the next game, and that was especially true in this case. The Knights were in a battle for first place in their division, and the playoff talk was only increasing with each passing game. Fleury also hadn't played in nearly two months, and nobody knew how sharp he would really be.

He was greeted with a standing ovation by the T-Mobile crowd as the Knights and Hurricanes skated onto the ice. Fleury quickly settled in and looked like his old self as the 'Canes put 11 shots on goal, with Marcus Kruger's the only one to elude him.

But the Knights tied it 1-1 early in the second period as Deryk Engelland beat Cam Ward. Trevor van Riemsdyk, who the Knights had taken from Chicago in the expansion draft before he and Kruger were traded to Carolina, scored to make it 2-1, only to have Reilly Smith tie it 12:48 into the second period.

It went to a shootout, and Phillip Di Giuseppe won it in the fifth round. The Knights got a point but it wasn't the way they were hoping to start the homestand.

"It was one game. I was a little excited maybe," Fleury said. "A little too much movement and stuff. I felt better as the game went on. The more shots I got, the more action I got. Obviously, there's still some stuff I want to work on. Shootouts, especially. I'm just trying to get better as we go."

Knights Coach Gerard Gallant said he could not blame Fleury for the Knights' four-game winning streak and Carolina's four-game losing streak both coming to an end.

"He's the reason we even got a point," Gallant said. "I thought he was excellent. He had some big saves for us to keep us in the game."

Ward, who earned his 300th career NHL victory, said doing it against Fleury made it extra special. "I thought (Fleury) had a heck of a game," the Carolina goalie said. "He's a guy that I respect a lot. I've been going against him for a lot of years. He's got a lot more wins than I do. It was great to see him back in the net. You never want to see a guy injured, and it was far too long."

Fleury was back, and now everyone's attention was on Thursday. There were plenty of stories about his days with the Penguins, how much he loved his former teammates and how there would be a flood of different emotions going into the puck-drop for Fleury. He also spoke well of his experience with his new team to date, how proud he was of what the Golden

Knights had accomplished so far, what lay ahead and what history was looming on the horizon.

"So many guys I played with for many years now. I know a little bit of what they like to do," Fleury said of facing his former team. "They know what I like to do. Hopefully, there's not too much thinking out there, and I can just play my usual game and try to do well against them."

The Penguins also weren't quite sure what to expect. Matt Murray, the team's goaltender who had learned at Fleury's side, said: "It will be interesting, for sure. It will be a bit surreal seeing him at the other end and competing against him. Obviously, it will be a lot of fun."

Sidney Crosby, the Penguins' captain, said he didn't know who had the advantage when it came to scoring against Fleury.

"When you shoot on a goalie for 12 years, I think he gets to know your tendencies pretty good," he said. "I'd like to think I know a few things about him, too. It'll be up to me to hopefully find those opportunities and up to us to generate those. Hopefully, it works out that I can get a couple of looks and see what I can do with them."

There was a higher-than-normal sense of anticipation prior to warmups. Visiting fans had become a regular presence at Golden Knights home games and they usually lined the glass near their team's bench. On this night, there was black and gold everywhere, virtually all wearing No. 29. They were not only behind the Penguins' bench, but behind the goal and around to the opposite side. Many were carrying signs expressing their love for Fleury.

The Golden Knights fans were also used to assembling by the glass for the warmups. Kids would bring signs saying it was their birthday, or their first NHL game, and would someone toss them a puck? This night the signs were for Fleury, and while the Penguins and Knights supporters were obviously on opposite sides when it came to their loyalties, when it came to Fleury, they were in lockstep when in their devotion for their "Flower."

Fleury and Murray met at center ice, gave each other a hug and wished each other luck. The other Penguins nodded toward their former teammate and pointed their sticks toward him in acknowledgment. There was great respect and love for Fleury and he had to feel weird about seeing the Penguins on the other side of the center red line.

Finally, the puck was dropped and it didn't take long for the fireworks to start. James Neal got the Knights the lead just 1:41 into the match as he beat Murray for a 1-0 lead. The Knights were at their best when they scored first and forced the other team to "chase the game", as hockey players and coaches liked to say.

But the Penguins were a veteran team and were back-to-back Stanley Cup champs for a reason. Panic was not in their lexicon, and veteran defenseman Ian Cole scored at the 12:04 mark to tie it 1-1.

It took on the feel of a playoff game as both teams played tight in front of their goaltenders, sweeping away rebounds and making smart plays to move the puck out of their zone. It was still tied heading toward the midway point of the third period when defenseman Jon Merrill broke the deadlock with a shot from the high slot on a nifty drop pass from Haula.

Merrill, who had starred at the University of Michigan, had been taken from New Jersey in the expansion draft. But he was having trouble cracking the lineup. However, when Luca Sbisa had sustained an injury two nights before, Gallant inserted

Merrill into the lineup and he scored his first goal of the season. He would take two penalties this night, but the Knights' penalty killing units along with Fleury bailed him out.

Trailing by a goal, the Penguins, as expected, made a strong push to get even. But the Knights continued to forecheck effectively and win the battles in their own end. They did not let Crosby, Evgeni Malkin, Phil Kessel or any of the other high-powered Pittsburgh threats beat them.

The final minutes seemed to take forever. But Fleury stayed strong and the Knights held on for the 2-1 win. Fleury was mobbed by his teammates afterward, and the 18,029 in the building rose as one and cheered the goaltender. Fleury admitted it was a bit surreal and definitely different.

"It's different. You didn't know what to expect," Fleury said after stopping 24 of the 25 shots the Penguins put on him. "I was quiet (during the game) I don't know why. I always yelled at (the Penguins) in practice and whatnot. Everyone played hard for 60 minutes, and I was very happy to get that win. I thank them for playing such a great game."

He was also happy to not have to answer anymore questions on what it would be like to face his former team. At least not for another couple of months.

While the narrative was to stay the same, the subject was about to change. The Florida Panthers were the Knights' next opponent. This time, Gallant, Smith and Marchessault would be asked about the Panthers. The focus would particularly be on Gallant, who everyone figured was out for revenge, given the way he and his former team parted company in the parking lot of PNC Arena in Raleigh, North Carolina, in late November of 2016.

If Gallant was still harboring any resentment, he wasn't showing it. And he sure wasn't saying it. He appreciated the Panthers giving him a chance to be an NHL head coach again, and he never held Dale Tallon responsible for what happened in the end. In fact, the day before the game the Panthers were practicing at City National Arena and Gallant and Tallon met and chatted for a while.

"There will definitely be something, but again, I'm there to coach my team the best I can and try and get two big points tonight," he said. "I had two and a half years in Florida, and I loved every minute of it. You move on and get ready for your next challenge."

Gallant went 96-65-25 with the Panthers, and he was a finalist for the Jack Adams Award as the NHL Coach of the Year in 2015-16 when he led Florida to a franchise-record 47 wins and 103 points. Gallant was fired Nov. 27, 2016, after opening the season 11-10-1.

"Tonight for me is another game. It's another two big points," Gallant said. "The only thing, I'll be looking out there and seeing a lot of players I'm real familiar with."

But his current players wanted to win this one for the man everyone calls "Turk", much the same way they all wanted to win for Fleury against Pittsburgh.

"I still feel bad about what happened to him when we were in Florida," Marchessault said of Gallant. "We feel like we let him down."

Fleury was getting the night off which was a good call on David Prior's part. Prior usually told Gallant who should play in net and Gallant had learned to trust Prior's instincts. "I don't know nothing about goaltending," Gallant said. "If Dave tells me to play a certain guy, I trust him."

Prior's thinking was that there could have been an emotional letdown after the win over the Penguins. Besides, the Tampa Bay Lightning were next up on the schedule after the struggling Panthers, and he wanted Fleury, who was still getting back his bearings, ready for Steven Stamkos, Nikita Kucherov, Victor Hedman and the rest of the Bolts.

Malcolm Subban got the start and it was a shaky one. The Panthers scored twice in the first 5:13 to take an early 2-0 lead, and everyone seemed to be playing with a hangover. Was it the "Vegas Flu" in reverse?

But the Knights rallied and tied the game late in the first period. Nate Schmidt had scored first at 6:39. Then Colin Miller followed with 2:40 left in the period. Now it was 2-2 and Subban had settled down.

Part of the Knights' game plan was to have the defense involved in the attack, and Schmidt and Miller were both excellent skaters who loved to join the rush. Both had been bottom-pairing D-men with their previous teams, Schmidt with Washington, Miller with Boston. But here the Knights had them as their top-four guys and working the power play.

Yet the game was still up for grabs in the third period. Then Haula took a pass from Marchessault, who was still on the ice during a line change, and Haula whipped it past James Reimer in the Florida goal to put the Knights in the lead 3-2. Marchessault and Neal added empty- net goals in the final 2:10 for a 5-2 victory that gave Gallant his revenge, wanted or not.

"It's like last game for (Fleury)," Marchessault said. "We wanted that win so much for him (and) I think tonight was the same thing. We wanted this win for Turk. It (the firing) just ended on such a terrible note. I think he's feeling pretty happy right now. It's our old team and we wanted to get that win. We have a good thing going on right here."

Good indeed. With the win, the Knights had pulled even with Los Angeles for first place in the Pacific Division, each team with 44 points. But perhaps their toughest test of the season awaited them two nights later. Tampa Bay had the NHL's best record at 24-8-2, and the Lightning were a lot like the Knights, only better. They played fast, struck quickly, had excellent goaltending and a mobile defense. And when they were on the power play, they were downright lethal.

They proved that in the first period as Stamkos and Vladislav Namestnikov scored with the man advantage to give Tampa a 2-0 lead. The Knights were one of the least penalized teams in the entire NHL, but against the Lightning, they were getting sent to the box.

Still, they had shown an ability to come back, and Neal and Marchessault led the comeback, Neal scoring his 17th of the year midway through the second period and Marchessault adding his 12th with 1:39 left. Ironically, both goals came on power plays, an area the Knights had not been particularly proficient in during the first part of the season. The Lightning was now the undisciplined team. A third-period penalty led to Haula putting Vegas ahead 3-2 just 4:42 in. But Hedman scored from the point with 3:52 left to tie it 3-3.

It appeared overtime was imminent. But Brayden Coburn was called for holding Neal's stick with 24 seconds left in regulation, and Shea Theodore would make the Lightning pay as he won it with a slap shot from the right point with just over two seconds remaining. Haula had won a battle for the puck and slid it to Marchessault who found Theodore uncovered. He let loose and Andrei Vasilevskiy, the Tampa goaltender, was slow to react.

"They're a phenomenal hockey team," Haula said of the Lightning. "But we kept going after them. I thought we outplayed them 5-on-5, and we never gave up, even when we fell behind."

Tampa coach John Cooper was impressed with his first look at the NHL's newest team.

"I understand we're coming in and there's 45 wins combined by the two teams going into the game," he said, explaining that he knew how big the game was, given it was only mid-December. "But for game 33 between a Western Conference team and an Eastern Conference team, it felt like that game could be played in May and not December."

Gallant said: "In my mind, Tampa is the best team in the league, and I thought we played fast and quick, and that's what you have to do against these guys. That's a great confidence builder for our group."

The Knights were now 3-1. The final contest in the five-game homestand would be against another high-powered opponent, the Washington Capitals, who had the NHL's top goal-scorer in Alex Ovechkin. It was a team George McPhee was very familiar with, since he built most of the core. Schmidt was also familiar with the Caps, having played for them prior to becoming a Golden Knight.

Christmas was only two days away and the team didn't want to spend the holiday on a bad note. So there was plenty of motivation for the Knights as the game got underway.

It took just 2:37 for the Knights to show how motivated they were as Alex Tuch beat Braden Holtby for an early 1-0 lead. Five minutes later, Oscar Lindberg scored to make it 2-0.

William Karlsson capped the scoring with 5:05 to go in the game for his 16th goal of the year. Karlsson had just 15 goals total in his two years with Columbus, so this was a big milestone for the center who obviously had found a home in Vegas.

Meanwhile, Schmidt had done a good job keeping an eye on Ovechkin, who was limited to just three shots on goal. Fleury stopped all 26 shots he faced and earned his first shutout with the Knights.

And as the players went their separate ways for Christmas, they did so with the knowledge they were tied for first place in the Pacific Division with 48 points and had a 23-9-2 record following a 4-1 homestand.

Gallant would say it was one of the turning points for the season.

"We beat some really good teams," he said. "I think we proved to ourselves we could play with the best teams in the league and it really helped our confidence as a group."

It would be a Merry Christmas, indeed.

12. Happy Holidays

Christmas is supposed to be about the spirit of giving, and the Golden Knights embraced giving back to the community.

Long before the horrific events of October 1, the team was already involved in numerous charitable ventures through its Golden Knights Foundation. Owner Bill Foley, a West Point graduate, had forged an alliance with the Folded Flag Foundation, an organization dedicated to supporting military families that lost loved ones in combat. The players also made visits in support of pediatric cancer patients and helped find homes for abandoned pets, in addition to other charitable activities.

One such venture, Pucks for Paws, raised over $20,000 as fans packed City National Arena to bid on 15 Pomeranian dogs that had been left abandoned in a truck near Las Vegas. The team had also donated $1 million to the Las Vegas Metropolitan Police Foundation in the aftermath of the October 1 shootings.

Virtually every NHL team raises money for charity through a 50/50 raffle. Fans purchase tickets before and during the game, usually until the end of the second period. At some point in the third period, the winning ticket number is announced, with half the money going to the lucky person holding the ticket and the team keeping the other half. With 41 home games, teams can raise hundreds of thousands of dollars for charity.

The Golden Knights put a little twist on the traditional 50/50 by forming a 51/49 raffle. They couched it by saying, "The odds are better in Vegas." The team would ultimately raise more than $1 million from the raffles for its foundation.

On the ice things were going well. The team was in first place when the season resumed December 27 in Anaheim, and after spotting the Ducks a 1-0 lead, the Knights answered with four unanswered goals, including William Karlsson's 17th of the year. The move by Gerard Gallant to move Karlsson up to the top line was proving to be a resounding success, and the 4-1 win after the Christmas break gave the team a little extra jump when they drove across town to face the Kings in Los Angeles the next night.

The games with the Kings were proving to be highly contested affairs as the Staples Center crowd was not shy at showing its disdain for the guys from Las Vegas. The Kings enjoyed a 1-0 lead going into the second period. But by now, opposing teams were well aware of the Knights' ability to show resiliency and come back. Sure enough, Jonathan Marchessault tied it 1-1 late in the second period, then Brendan Leipsic scored his first goal of the year a little past the midway point of the third period to give the Knights a 2-1 lead.

Leipsic, a five-foot, ten-inch winger, had been selected from Toronto in the expansion draft and he played a hard, fast game. He was not shy of making contact and he always gave an honest effort. Like Brad Hunt, the undersized defenseman, Leipsic found himself in and out of the lineup, but he never complained and his teammates were fond of him. He had been shooting into hard luck all year and he probably should have had 10 goals by now. But he would either hit the post or the crossbar, just miss the net, or the opposing goaltender would rob him.

But the Kings were a resilient bunch themselves and Drew Doughty tied it with 4:33 to play. It went to overtime and the Knights won it on David Perron's goal, as Reilly Smith set him up in front of Jonathan Quick and Perron got the better of Quick for the 3-2 game-winner. It was the sixth straight win for the Knights and they were now all alone in first place in the Pacific Division with 52 points.

And as the team prepared to end the 2017 portion of its schedule with a New Year's Eve matinee at T-Mobile Arena against the Maple Leafs, they did so as one of the NHL's elite teams. Only Tampa Bay had more wins (26) and points (56) than the Golden Knights. And who would have predicted that?

T-Mobile had a ton of Toronto fans in the building, and why not? A chance to see the Leafs and party on the Strip to ring in the new year? Made all the sense in the world.

On the roster for Mike Babcock was old friend Calvin Pickard, who had been called up from the Leafs' AHL farm team, the Toronto Marlies. The Marlies were one of three AHL teams that shared a city with an NHL team, Winnipeg and Chicago being the others. However, you could argue that Ontario, the Kings' AHL team, wasn't that far a drive from Los Angeles, the stifling freeway traffic notwithstanding.

The Knights got off to a 3-0 lead, beating Freddie Andersen three times in the first 13:24. For a moment it appeared Pickard would be summoned to face his old mates. But Babcock stuck with his starter, and the Leafs rallied to pull within 4-3 just 27 seconds into the third period as Auston Matthews scored his second of the game.

However, this would be Karlsson's day. He had scored the second and fourth goals for Vegas, and with the Knights leading 5-3 late in the contest, he finished the day with a great hustle play, diving for a loose puck near the right face-off circle. And as he was falling, he swiped his stick at the puck and deposited it into the empty net with 36 seconds remaining for the first hat trick in team history, sealing the Knights' 6-3 win.

"It was pretty unreal," Karlsson said. "You dream about that your whole life. I don't think I've ever skated so fast in my life. I really wanted it. I just threw myself at it, and it was a good feeling to see it go into the net."

The Knights had now won seven straight, extending their lead in the division and finishing the month with an amazing 11-2 record. They were not only the talk of the hockey world, the entire sports world was starting to take notice.

Expansion teams aren't supposed to be this successful this soon. Obviously, no one was expecting a hockey version of the 1962 New York Mets or the 1976 Tampa Bay Buccaneers, the standards for first-year ineptitude. Nor were these Knights expected to be the 1974-75 Washington Capitals, which was the worst expansion team in the sport's history, winning just eight games.

The rules for the expansion draft had been set up to prevent such a scenario. But 26 wins and the best record in the Western Conference on New Year's Day 2018? How was this possible?

The players and their coach knew.

"We knew there was a lot of talent," forward James Neal said. "A lot of us had played against each other and we have a great goaltender in Flower (Marc-Andre Fleury), who gives us a chance to win every night. I think what has everyone surprised was how quickly we were able to come together as a team. But I could tell back in training camp that we were going to be successful. Everyone got along. There were no egos. Everybody was working hard and we had a great coaching staff."

Gallant said the players' willingness to work hard and play for each other was the primary reason for the team's success to date.

"All I ever asked was that they come to the rink, put in the work and have fun," he said. "They've done exactly that."

Karlsson wasn't the only Knights player having a career season. Haula had taken advantage of his opportunity too, and he was one goal away from equaling his career high of 15 which was set two years before in Minnesota.

The Knights were looking to build on their seven-game winning streak when they hosted Nashville in the first game of 2018 for the franchise. Their first meeting had ended in an exciting shootout win in Music City in early December with Malcolm Subban in goal. Now they were in Sin City and Fleury was between the pipes for the second of the three meetings between the teams.

More than midway through the second period, Reilly Smith scored to break a scoreless tie and give the Knights the lead. Whenever the Knights scored first they were 17-0-1.

A minute thirty-one later, Shea Theodore made it 2-0, beating Pekka Rinne, the Predators' outstanding goaltender. Meanwhile, Fleury was stopping everything Nashville threw at him. He would stop all 28 shots that he faced, and Marchessault finished the 3-0 win with an empty-net goal with 2:23 to play. It was the eighth straight victory for the Knights and a perfect start to 2018.

"Our goaltending has been unbelievable all season," Gallant said of Fleury. "He's the face of our franchise and he kept us in it. He stood on his head and gave us a chance to get the lead."

When would the Knights lose again? They were on a roll the way a craps player kept making passes at the table. But they were back on the road, and the streak ended two nights later in St. Louis, a 2-1 loss to the Blues. But the team almost lost one of its staff that night.

Goaltending coach David Prior complained of shortness of breath and tightness in his chest before the game. Trainer Kyle Moore quickly got Prior onto a table and called for help from the Blues.

An ambulance is required at every NHL game and one was just pulling into the Scottrade Center. The 61-year-old Prior was having a heart attack, and he was quickly loaded into the ambulance and rushed to a nearby hospital.

"My body has grown its own collateral bypasses under the artery that rerouted blood and prevented a heart attack prior to that," Prior told Sports Illustrated. "It's not lost on me how extremely fortunate I was to escape that situation."

Prior, who had been the unsung hero in navigating the team through its goaltender injury dilemma, was lucky beyond words. His heart had not sustained any damage, though it was discovered that two of his coronary arteries were blocked to the point that his heart had stopped beating. He was fortunate to have been within arm's reach of medical attention. Had he been anywhere else, he probably would have died.

Four stents were inserted to reopen the arteries and he was discharged from the hospital 36 hours after being admitted. Amazingly, he would return to work two days later, though in a reduced capacity.

The Blues posted a 2-1 win, though Haula equalled his career-best by scoring his 15th goal of the season which tied the game 1-1 at 9:23 of the second period. The Knights had a couple of great opportunities late to tie it and force overtime, but Carter Hutton was tremendous in the St. Louis net, and he helped preserve the victory and snap Vegas' eight-game win streak.

It was on to Chicago to face the struggling Blackhawks. The team had won the Stanley Cup just three years ago. But they bore no resemblance to that group. They were mired in last place in the Central Division. Corey Crawford, their starting goaltender, was out with a concussion. Several of the team's veterans were underachieving and there was already talk that perhaps changes were coming in the off-season if things didn't turn around quickly.

The United Center is a cavernous barn seating 19,717. It is a loud place, starting when the fans try to drown out Jim Cornelison, the accomplished national anthem singer who might be the best in the entire NHL. When he gets to the line "that our flag was still there" and points at the American flag hanging in the rafters, somehow the decibel level goes up even higher.

The Knights had searched for their own Jim Cornelison, and after having several different anthem singers early on, they settled on Carnell Johnson, who possessed a deep, rich baritone voice and worked as a singing gondolier at the Venetian Hotel and Casino. Johnson was one of over 600 applicants who had submitted tapes in the hopes of landing the gig. And the first time he sang at T-Mobile Arena, the fans loved him. He was a big hit on social media and some tweeted: "We've found our anthem singer."

Many teams' fan bases will yell a word during the anthem. In Las Vegas, whenever the line "gave proof through the night" came around, the fans would yell "NIGHT" in unison though they really meant "KNIGHT". It became a tradition that quickly caught on, and Johnson, who would eventually be the regular anthem singer, would pause when he came to the word to let the fans shout it before continuing on with the rest of the anthem.

The performance by Cornelison seemed to fire up the visitors more than the home team. Alex Tuch and Marchessault scored to give the Knights a 2-0 first-period lead, and 5:54 into the second period the Knights led 3-1 as Karlsson scored his 21st of the season. But the Blackhawks showed some rare moxie, rallying to take control of the game and lead 4-3 as Jonathan Toews beat Malcolm Subban 30 seconds into the third period.

However, the Knights had learned not to get discouraged when they let the other team back into the game. They tied it 4-4 as Cody Eakin beat starter Jeff Glass at the 5:33 mark. Smith then scored the game winner with just over six minutes to go. He had knocked the puck away from defenseman Connor Murphy and broke in all alone, then scored on Glass to the stick side. It was a heady play by Smith and it spoke to how seriously he took his defensive responsibilities. If he had been on the other side of the blue line, he doesn't make that play.

There was good news and bad news on the injury front. Forward Will Carrier had returned to the lineup the night before against St. Louis after missing 16 games with a lower-body injury. The bad news was that the Knights were losing defenseman Luca Sbisa again after he injured his hand during a second-period fight with John Hayden. Sbisa had been out for nine games with an upper-body injury. Now he was headed back to the injured-reserve list.

They were also without Pierre-Edouard Bellemare, the anchor of the fourth line and the team's best penalty killer. But Bellemare wasn't injured. He and his wife Hannah were celebrating the birth of their first child, a son, Leandre Lian, while the team was in St. Louis. He would rejoin the team Sunday when the New York Rangers visited T-Mobile Arena.

The Rangers figured to have a lot of support in Las Vegas. Many ex-New Yorkers lived in town and their hockey loyalties remained with the Broadway Blueshirts. Sure enough, the chants of "Go Knights Go!" was met with an equally loud "Let's Go Rangers!" chant. At times it felt like you were in Madison Square Garden, especially after Mika Zibanejad beat Fleury 13:05 into the match to give the Rangers a 1-0 lead.

Even one of the notorious Garden traditions surfaced as a clandestine Ranger fan whistled and his fellow fans responded with "Potvin Sucks," a taunt aimed at Islanders Hall of Fame defenseman Denis Potvin who in 1979 knocked Rangers forward Ulf Nilsson out of the game with a hit that resulted in Nilsson breaking his ankle. Every time Potvin touched the puck, Ranger fans would yell "Potvin Sucks!" and would do so each time the Isles and Rangers met until Potvin retired in 1988.

After that, the tradition continued as a sing-song chord would be played by the Garden organist, followed by the chant. And after the organist stopped playing the chords leading up to the chant, a fan or fans would whistle the tune to set up the chant. It continues to this very day, even though Potvin, currently a television analyst for the Florida Panthers, hasn't played in 30 years.

Weirdness aside, the Knights tied the game late in the first period as James Neal scored to make it 1-1 against Andrej Pavelec, who was playing in place of Henrik Lundqvist. Midway through the third period, Karlsson scored on a one-timer after Smith set him up for what would prove to be the game-winner, as the Knights took a 2-1 lead. Fleury made 28 saves, and with the NHL mandatory week break upon them, the Knights had a 29-10-2 record. They would have a chance to make history on an upcoming four-game road trip through the South.

13. Chasing History

The Rangers had a large presence in T-Mobile Arena on January 7, but it paled in comparison to the orange wave that represented the Edmonton Oilers when the Golden Knights' season resumed on January 13. There were 18,351 in the building, the largest crowd in the brief history of the franchise, and half the building was made up of Oilers fans.

Their team was having a lousy season. But Connor McDavid was still worth seeing, so the Oilers fans invested hundreds, and, in some cases, a couple of thousand dollars to watch their captain, who was turning 21 years old this day. He certainly wasn't the first guy to celebrate that milestone in Vegas.

But McDavid wasn't going on a drunken binge or spending his night celebrating in a bunch of strip clubs or gambling into the wee hours. He was here to work and his teammates fell in lockstep, taking a 1-0 lead eight minutes in as Patrick Maroon beat Fleury. During the ice maintenance shortly afterward, the fans serenaded McDavid with "Happy Birthday." It wasn't Marilyn Monroe singing to John F. Kennedy but it would suffice.

As expected, the Knights battled back and took a 2-1 lead late in the second period as Karlsson scored on a one-timer after Smith had scored midway through the period to tie it. But the Knights have also shown an ability to squander leads in the third period, and Drake Caggiula tied it 2-2 just 3:29 into the third as the defense broke down and left him alone in front of Fleury.

It went to overtime and for the first time this season, the Knights failed to either win or get it to the shootout as defenseman Darnell Nurse finished off a 3-on-1 rush by beating Fleury. And the Oilers left Vegas a 3-2 winner. The Knights had played 13 division games and were 11-2, with both losses coming to Edmonton.

It was time to hit the road and Nashville was the first stop. The Predators were playing well and along with the Knights were among the best teams in the Western Conference. It figured to be a hard-fought contest when the Knights stepped onto the ice at Bridgestone Arena on January 16 to kick off the four-game trip. Vegas expected to see Pekka Rinne in goal. But the Nashville netminder was under the weather and unable to play. The team had called up Juuse Saros from their AHL affiliate in Milwaukee after he was getting some work in during the Predators' mandatory break, and he was in net.

He would face 41 shots and stopped every one of them as Kevin Fiala's third-period goal against Fleury stood up to give Nashville a 1-0 victory, handing the Knights their second straight loss.

The outcome of the game wasn't the only loss. Tomas Nosek was injured in the first period and would be out 12 games with an upper-body injury.

It was on to Tampa and a rematch with the Lightning. The first meeting was a spirited battle and the same was expected at Amalie Arena the night of January 18. For Fleury, Neal and

Gallant, it was a building they would become familiar with as the city was scheduled to host the NHL All-Star Game the following weekend. Gallant would coach the Pacific Division All-Stars with Fleury and Neal among the 11 players on the roster.

But nobody was thinking about All-Star Games. Suddenly, people were speculating that this might be a preview of the Stanley Cup Final. Crazy as it seemed, the Golden Knights were in the Cup conversation even though half the regular season remained to be played.

When owner Bill Foley had been asked the day the team was awarded its franchise how long would it take to contend for a championship, his response was, "Well, I hope we can be in the playoffs by our third year and compete for the Stanley Cup in Year Six." Now that plan was accelerated. The phrase "Cup in 1" was starting to be bandied about on social media, and while it still seemed far-fetched, a lot of fans were jumping on board to that notion.

It took just 56 seconds for the Knights to show how important this game was as Neal beat Andrei Vasilevskiy for a 1-0 lead. Nate Schmidt made it 2-0 with less than four minutes remaining in the first period, and Fleury appeared to be on his game.

Before the match, Gallant reminded his players how important it was to stay out of the penalty box. The Lightning had a great power play and not everyone got the memo. Karlsson, one of the least-penalized players in the NHL, took a tripping penalty midway through the second period, and sure enough Tampa capitalized as Andrej Palat scored to cut the lead to 2-1.

Karlsson took another tripping penalty in the third period but the Knights were able to kill that one off. He redeemed himself a bit by scoring the final goal 18 seconds into the third period in a 4-1 victory, and he now had 24 for the season, a remarkable number. The Knights had swept the season series, and with a 30-11-2 record and 62 points, not only were they the best team in the entire Western Conference, they were just two points from owning the best record in all of hockey.

The next night, against the Florida Panthers, the Knights had an opportunity to tie for the most points in the NHL. It was Gallant's first visit to the BB&T Center since he was fired on November 27, 2016, and he was trying to treat it like another game. But that was virtually impossible. So many people knew him and wanted to say hello and congratulate him for the job he had done with the Golden Knights, he couldn't avoid the awkwardness of it all.

"I enjoyed my time here," Gallant said before the game. "It was great. We had successful seasons and played real well and the fans were real good to me. It's too bad what happened."

The Panthers did acknowledge Gallant's return on the video screen, and the fans stood and gave him a nice ovation, which Gallant appreciated. He would have appreciated a victory more. But it wasn't to be as the Panthers' Aaron Ekblad scored 40 seconds into overtime to give the home team a 4-3 win.

The trip wrapped up in Raleigh, North Carolina, where Gallant had been fired. He was hoping for a better result this time around and he would get it as Bellemare scored 2:55 into the contest to give the Knights an early 1-0 lead. The Knights scored twice more on goals from Colin Miller on a power play and Marchessault at even strength to chase Hurricanes goalie

Scott Darling 12:59 into the contest. Cam Ward mopped up, but Neal and Leipsic beat him and the Knights cruised to a 5-1 win.

It was the team's 31st win in its inaugural season and its 66th point overall. And when the NHL standings came out Monday morning, the Vegas Golden Knights had the most points of any team in the league.

In 2016 the NHL decided its All-Star Game needed a makeover. Taking a page from its rule book, which called for 3-on-3 in overtime, the league decided to try a format that pitted division vs. division, playing 3-on-3 with $1 million going to the winner. Each division had an 11-man roster and it would hopefully restore a little integrity in what had become a farce of an event. What did the NHL have to lose?

The first attempt came in Nashville and it was a huge hit. It didn't hurt that John Scott was the hero, having helped the Pacific Division win it after he had been traded from Arizona to Montreal, and then demoted to the Canadiens' AHL affiliate in St. John, Newfoundland. But the fans voted Scott in and though the NHL wasn't happy about it, it allowed Scott to play. He wound up being the game's Most Valuable Player.

The following year in Los Angeles, the Metropolitan Division beat the Pacific 4-3 with Philadelphia's Wayne Simmonds the MVP. Now the game was in Tampa and the Golden Knights were well represented by goaltender Marc-Andre Fleury and forward James Neal, along with coach Gerard Gallant. Many felt William Karlsson deserved to be in the game. Same for Jonathan Marchessault. Both were having great seasons and would have been honored to play had they been selected. But with only 11 spots and each team having to be represented, the math simply didn't work.

Sometimes players would just as soon pass on participating in an event like the All-Star Game. They would rather spend the time with their families and use the break to heal up. But Fleury had missed 25 games already and he wouldn't turn down any opportunity to play. Neal had played in the All-Star Game in Nashville as a member of the Predators and he had a blast. Gallant had coached in the 2016 event as the Atlantic Division coach and he, too, enjoyed the experience.

With Fleury and Calgary's Mike Smith sharing the goaltender chores, the Pacific won the championship game, beating the Atlantic 5-2.

"It felt great to watch our players," Gallant said. "They represented our organization real well, and it makes it fun when the guys represent the organization. To see those guys play well and win a championship, it was good."

Prior to the All-Star Game, the Knights split a pair of home games, defeating Columbus 6-3 as Karlsson scored twice against his former team and Erik Haula scored his career-best 16th goal. Two nights later, the New York Islanders defeated the Knights 2-1 and swept the season series. Still, they were 32-12-4 and leading their division. They were still tops in the conference, and their 68 points was second in the entire NHL. Only the Lightning had more with 71 points.

They were also a win away from tying the NHL record for most victories by an expansion team. But it wasn't going to be so easy to reach that mark. The team was about to embark on its longest and toughest road trip of the season — six games in 10 days, in two countries, across all four time zones.

It began in Calgary, with the first meeting against the Flames. Glen Gulutzan, the Calgary coach, was familiar to Las Vegans, having coached the ECHL's Wranglers and having served as their original general manager. Deryk Engelland, who had played for Gulutzan, first with the Wranglers, then the last couple of years with the Flames, was returning to Calgary for the first time and was excited about returning. Engelland was having the best season of his NHL career and he credited Gulutzan for helping him get there.

"It started in Calgary," Engelland said. "Gully gave me the opportunity to play more and it really helped my confidence. And it's been the same here. I'm getting more opportunities, and it's been a great experience so far."

The Flames were trying to stay in the playoff race and this was a big game for them, even though it was only January 30. They couldn't afford to fall too much further back if they were serious about contending for the postseason. And when Matthew Tkachuk scored with 1:17 left in the second period to break a 1-1 tie and put the Flames in the lead, things were looking pretty good for them. Mike Smith was playing well in the Calgary net and the Knights were struggling to get the puck by him.

With time winding down, the Knights caught a huge break. Micheal Ferland was looking to clear the puck out of his zone, but he tried to clear it across the ice in front of his own net. Haula was at the right post and the puck wound up on his stick. Before a surprised Smith could react, the puck was in the net and the game was tied 2-2.

"I'm still amazed at what happened," Haula said after the game. "Somehow the puck ended up on my stick, so I guess I got a little lucky there."

But it would get worse for the Flames. They lost the face-off at center ice and Karlsson got the puck to Marchessault who broke in alone and beat Smith 10 seconds after Haula had scored to give the Knights a 3-2 lead. David Perron added an empty-net goal 43 seconds later to complete an improbable comeback and give the Knights a 4-2 win and a record-tying 33rd victory.

It was one of the team's best wins all season, and Gallant tried to keep it in perspective.

"It's great for the franchise, but there's a lot of hockey left to play," Gallant said. "The guys kept working and we got a little lucky. But it's a big two points and a great way to start the road trip."

It was on to chilly Winnipeg, where the temperature was well below zero and winter had put its bite on Manitoba's capital. The Knights were going to have a chance to etch their name in the history books with a win, and they knew it would take a big effort to beat the Jets, who were starting to surge themselves as one of the top teams in the Western Conference, along with Nashville. The Jets had one of the game's rising stars in forward Patrik Laine, and there was a group of talented players in Mark Scheifele, Bryan Little and Dustin Byfuglien. But Scheifele would not play on February 1 and his absence was noteworthy.

Unlike their last meeting, which was a wide-open affair that the Jets won 7-4 back on December 1, this one was a lot tighter, with lots of close checking. The Jets saw a 1-0 first-period lead become a 2-1 deficit in the second period. But Kyle Connor scored with 2:36 to play to tie it 2-2 and force overtime.

There was also a bit of controversy as James Neal attempted to bat a puck out of the air only to hit Winnipeg goalie Connor Hellebuyck in the head before Haula scored in the second period to give the Knights a 2-1 lead. The play didn't draw a penalty and it left Jets coach Paul Maurice fuming. He challenged, citing goaltender interference but the appeal was denied.

Maurice was even angrier after David Perron won it in overtime with 1:03 remaining. The Jets had three chances to win prior to Perron's heroics. But they hit the post once, and Fleury managed to keep it out of his net the two other times. Schmidt had been denied by Hellebuyck at the other end during OT, so both teams had great opportunities.

And as the Knights congratulated Fleury and Perron, they did so having made hockey history. In just their 50th game as a franchise, the Vegas Golden Knights had 34 wins.

"Once we got to 30 wins, we knew we were going to get there," Perron said of the record. "But it's important that we keep looking at things day-to-day and keep trying to get better."

As was the case in Calgary when his team equalled the mark, Gallant wasn't ready to celebrate. "It's great. But it doesn't mean a whole lot right now to be honest with you," Gallant said. "We're just trying to battle to get two points every night. But at the end of the season we'll look back on it and be happy."

More important to Gallant was the fact his team was 2-0 on the six-game road trip and was hoping to keep things going as it landed in Minnesota for a match with the Wild the next night. The Wild had Las Vegas' Jason Zucker on their roster, and he was having a career year himself. While not born in Nevada, Zucker moved to town when he was a youngster and grew up playing roller hockey at the Crystal Palace roller skating rink. He switched to ice hockey, would represent the USA in the World Junior Championships, earned a scholarship to the University of Denver, then got drafted by the Wild in the second round of the 2010 NHL draft.

Zucker was glad to see Las Vegas supporting the NHL and he was happy for the Knights' success, especially after the events of October 1, followed by how the team helped the city heal. But he also wanted to keep up his good play. He was a restricted free agent and he and his wife Carly had become parents at the start of the season to a baby boy. A good season would help his case to stay in the Twin Cities.

The Super Bowl was in town when the Knights headed to the Xcel Energy Center, with fans of the New England Patriots and Philadelphia Eagles taking over Minneapolis. Fortunately for the Knights they were playing in St. Paul where the Super Bowl's reach wasn't as great. Besides, it was well below zero and who wanted to brave the frigid temperatures to go travel to watch hockey?

The natives were another story. The Wild sold out every game and they billed themselves the "State of Hockey" with good reason. Minnesota's hockey tradition runs deep. Herb Brooks, the coach of the USA's Miracle on Ice at the 1980 Winter Olympics, has a statue outside the X, as the locals call the arena. The Minnesota State Boys High School Hockey Championship is considered a must-see event.

For the Knights, they wouldn't be lingering around for the Super Bowl anyway. They were headed to Washington after the game with the Wild and they would watch the game at their D.C hotel. As it turned out, they couldn't get to the nation's capital fast enough. The Wild jumped out to a 3-0 lead, and despite Haula scoring his 20th of the year to cut the deficit to 3-1, the Knights were never in it. Minnesota posted a 5-2 victory. Schmidt, who had played with Haula at the University of Minnesota and who had scored the other Vegas goal, was ready to get on the plane and have his homecoming in Washington.

Schmidt wouldn't be the only person with the Knights who was coming back. George McPhee, who had built the Capitals before his contract was not renewed after the 2014 season, also was returning to his former workplace.

Schmidt talked about the good memories he had playing for the Capitals and how coach Barry Trotz gave him some good advice after the Knights selected him in the expansion draft.

"He told me to embrace the opportunity and enjoy it," Schmidt told a scrum of reporters prior to the afternoon game on February 4. "He said make it a positive experience, and Barry was right. It's been a blast so far."

McPhee didn't carry on a regular dialogue with reporters. But he did talk about his time in Washington for the team's website.

"It's different coming in as the opponent," McPhee said. "It's uncomfortable in some ways, pulling for one group while watching another. But there are some nice memories."

Afternoon games can be tough for both teams. Hockey players, like most athletes, are creatures of habit. And the vast majority of NHL games are played in the evening. That means your game-day routine consists of getting up, going to the rink for the morning skate, returning home or back to your hotel, taking a nap, heading back to the rink and playing. But afternoon games take the morning skate and pregame nap out of the equation. Instead, you get up, have breakfast, go to the rink and play. It sounds easy but in reality it can be a challenge.

Of course, both teams have to go through it, just like they both have to skate on the same ice.

The Capitals struck first 7:22 in to lead 1-0. But Ryan Carpenter tied it with less than four minutes to go in the period. Carpenter had been waived by San Jose and picked up by the Knights off waivers. He was a blue-collar player who gave an honest effort, played both ends of the ice and didn't back away from a physical challenge. He had done more sitting than playing since his arrival and this was just his sixth game.

But when Will Carrier injured his shoulder on his second shift and had to leave the game, Carpenter found himself playing more. He had 12:27 in ice time and he would play a critical role in the outcome.

The Capitals had a 3-2 lead 52 seconds into the third period as Nicklas Backstrom scored. The Knights pushed to get the equalizer against Philipp Grubauer, who was in goal for Braden Holtby that day. Eventually, persistence paid off as Reilly Smith got his second of the game to tie it 3-3 midway through the period. It was his 16th of the year, one more than his entire total in 2016-17. And with just over five minutes to play, Carpenter set up Alex Tuch for what would be the game-winning goal, finding him alone in front, where he beat Grubauer.

Now came the tricky part. The Knights were clinging to a one-goal lead. Fleury was playing well in net. But the Caps had Alex Ovechkin, Evgeny Kuznetsov, John Carlson and Backstrom, all of whom were more than capable of scoring.

The Capitals were pushing hard for the equalizer. The Knights, who had been without Carrier since early in the first period, were undoubtedly fatigued. This was their third game in four days and now they were short a forward.

Gallant sent out Carpenter along with Bellemare and Tuch to try and keep the Caps from tying it. With about 40 seconds remaining, Backstrom saw Brett Connolly wide open at the left circle half-boards. Backstrom, one of the game's great passers, sent the puck across and if it reached Connolly's stick, it might have meant overtime. But Carpenter read the play and was in position to reach out and get his stick blade on the puck just before Connolly could tee it up and let it rip. The Knights would hold on for a 4-3 win, and that postgame Super Bowl party at the team's hotel just got a lot more festive.

"I feel grateful to having been able to contribute," Carpenter said. "I was just trying to make a good read on the play and I managed to get my stick on the puck before it got to (Connolly).

"When I got here after waivers, I didn't really know what to expect. But it's a great group of guys, and I love being here."

The win guaranteed the Knights no worse than a .500 result on the six-game road trip as they were now 3-1. Two stops remained, starting Tuesday in Pittsburgh. For Fleury, it was the most anticipated away game of his career.

14. Welcome Back Fleury

If you thought Marc-Andre Fleury was loved in Las Vegas, it paled in comparison to the devotion he was showered with in Pittsburgh. From 2003 to 2017, he was a huge part of the Penguins. He had three Stanley Cup championship rings, and he was one of the most popular athletes in the city. That's saying something when you consider the football Steelers and the baseball Pirates.

The Knights chose to wait until Monday to travel to the Steel City, having done some team bonding the night before while watching the Philadelphia Eagles defeat the New England Patriots for the team's first Super Bowl title. In Pittsburgh they weren't celebrating the Eagles' triumph. The Steelers had six Vince Lombardi Trophies to their credit. So as far as Pittsburghers were concerned, Philly had a long way to go before it could claim any sort of Keystone State bragging rights.

Vegas headed over to PPG Paints Arena for practice. They were met by a huge throng of media who wanted to talk to Fleury, and, to a lesser extent, James Neal, David Perron and Deryk Engelland, who also had played for the Penguins. Fleury, always gracious with his time, tried to accommodate everyone. He held court in front of his locker, and with the throng nearly eight deep, he had to repeat himself more than he probably would have liked.

The team probably should have asked him if he would have preferred to have a room for himself, complete with a chair and a microphone where he could relax, be comfortable and enjoy the process. But it never happened.

Like virtually all athletes, Fleury is superstitious. One of those superstitions is that he doesn't do interviews on game days. Those who had covered him in Pittsburgh knew that, so this was their one shot to talk to him, to find out his thoughts about returning to the city where he had experienced his success in pro hockey.

"It's definitely weird," Fleury said as he held court with media. "I want to win the game, but I don't want to block everything out either. It's my first game back here. I want to enjoy the moment. It's the first time I've been through it and I don't think there's anything that prepares you for it.

"I have had such great support here over the years, through the good and through the bad. The people have always been very supportive of me, always cheering me on. So I think it will be fun. It was my home for so long, from the neighbors to the restaurants; it brings back memories over the years, fun times."

Gerard Gallant knew there was nothing he could say to sell the idea that for his team this was just another game.

"Marc's a true pro," Gallant said. "I'm sure it's going to be emotional for him, but he played here a long time. He's got three Stanley Cup championships. He's got a lot of friends here. So it'll be a lot of fun. It's another game for us, but for Marc it's a big game."

In the Penguins' locker room things were equally awkward heading into the much-anticipated meeting.

"I'm sure it'll be weird for him," Penguins captain Sidney Crosby said. "But he's going to get a great ovation, and once you get into the game you get competitive, and you have fun with it and try to put the puck past him.

"There's always motivation when you play against friends and former teammates, especially in the position we're in and what happened there (in Vegas). We want to make sure we find a way to win this one."

Fleury's impact on Pittsburgh reached far beyond his goal crease. Ed Graney, the Las Vegas Review-Journal's award-winning columnist, found that out first-hand as he visited the Sto-Ken-Rox Boys & Girls Club in McKees Rocks, one of the city's most economically depressed areas. It was the place Fleury chose to help when he could have gone anywhere else or written a check and hoped the problem would go away. Instead, he wanted to leave something that would have permanence and provide hope.

"We still can't believe what the Fleury family did for our community," Kevin Nicholson, executive director of the club, told Graney. "We have more kids now than we ever had — 120 to 130 a day — and all of what he gave allowed them to be more active. Marc did this for all the right reasons. It's something that will be here for a very long time. It's a tough place for a lot of these kids. Not a lot of money. Even the younger ones who might not know who No. 29 is. We teach them. All of this was very needed."

Graney wrote in his column: "At one point Tuesday, a minivan pulled up and a seven-year-old boy bounded from the front seat, heading for another day of hockey inside Rink 29."

"The kids needed something like this in the neighborhood," said his mother, Casey Bayer. "They deserve nice things to happen for them. Everyone loves Fleury here."

Graney's column continued: "In a town of 6,000 that never really recovered from the collapse of the steel industry, where the streets are narrow along the south banks of the Ohio River, they will share stories about the famous goalie who before leaving his adopted home, helped the most precious of things — its children."

"It's what is important, yes?" Fleury said. "To give something back that will last."

And while none of the Boys & Girls Club members or their parents could afford to welcome back Fleury in person, they were supportive from afar, some six miles away. But there was no shortage of people, some who paid over $1,000, to come say "hello" and welcome Fleury back on a cold February night.

Long before the pregame warmups, the fans gathered, many holding signs expressing their love and admiration for Fleury. And as he led the Knights onto the ice, he couldn't help but notice the support. They chanted "Fleury, Fleury, Fleury" as he tried to focus on getting ready to play.

He had never experienced anything quite like it. And with his family, his agent and friends watching from a suite, Fleury prepared to settle in as the puck was dropped at 7:08 p.m.

Evgeni Malkin had taken a slashing penalty just 1:07 into the contest, and the Knights quickly took advantage with William Karlsson scoring on the power play to stake Fleury to a 1-0 lead. Neal made it 2-0 at the 6:34 mark, and it looked like Fleury's teammates were going to deliver and get him a big win on this emotional night.

During the first TV timeout in the first period the Penguins played a one-minute, 45-second video in tribute to Fleury.That was followed by a lengthy standing ovation. The cameras caught Fleury tearing up a little and as he said afterward, "I'm glad I had my mask on."

But the Penguins weren't about to roll over. Ryan Reaves scored to cut the deficit to 2-1 at 11:08 of the second period. Ironically, Reaves would become Fleury's teammate in 17 days. The goal seemed to energize the Penguins and their crowd. Ian Cole tied it 2-2 with 2:36 to go in the period and Jake Guentzel put the Pens in the lead, 3-2, 1:16 later.

Now in control, the Penguins stepped on the gas. Malkin and Kessel scored 3:11 apart in the third period as the lead grew to 5-2. Ryan Carpenter and Jonathan Marchessault made it interesting as their goals on Matt Murray cut it to 5-4 with 7:59 to play. But the Knights were unable to get even and come away with at least a point. Fleury played well, especially given the circumstances, finishing with 33 saves. But he had to settle for a season split with his former team.

As always, he took things in stride.

"I didn't know what to expect," he told reporters afterward. "In warmups I had goosebumps. Before the game, people had signs and kind words. It's a night I won't forget. Except maybe the score.

"It was just amazing; the support I've gotten over the years here is just incredible. I thank everybody for all these years and once again for showing up tonight with such great support."

As for the first-period video tribute, he appreciated the gesture.

"They always do a good job with these (videos)," he said. "A lot of good memories. A lot of good years. It just brought some fun memories."

He was glad to put it behind him and get on with trying to get his team into the playoffs.

"There was lots going on, lots of happiness, and emotions, and stress," Fleury said. "But it was worth it."

Murray said of the game: "It was what I think everybody expected it to be. It was an emotional, pretty free-flowing game. They're a really good team. They're tough to play against. We had to give it our best to get the two points."

"It's a tough loss," Gallant said. "We played a real good 30 minutes, and then we sort of backed off. That's why they're the Stanley Cup champs. They can create good plays. I thought the first 30 we played real well.

"We didn't skate, we didn't work hard enough and our gaps were bad. When you give the room to make plays in the neutral zone, with their speed, they're going to attack you. I thought we backed off too much and gave them too many odd-man rushes."

His teammates were disappointed they didn't get their goaltender the desired result.

"Obviously the city loves him, guys love him, we certainly love him here and we're happy to have him," said Neal. "I just wish we had a better effort for him."

Karlsson said: "There was a lot of emotion. I can't imagine how Fleury was feeling, especially during that tribute video. I'm not happy that we didn't win for him."

It was snowing as the Knights headed for the airport Wednesday morning and the long flight to San Jose. Their flight would be delayed leaving Pittsburgh, and they didn't reach California until late in the afternoon. So far the team had encountered few if any difficulties in their travels, thanks to Rick Braunstein, the team's director of travel services who was an experienced hand at dealing with all sorts of potential pitfalls. He always had a Plan B and a Plan C if necessary, if Plan A didn't work. He was never without his laptop computer and if there were any issues, questions or problems, the answer or solution was usually just a click or two away.

As was the case with all division games, this one was important. Yes, the Knights still led the Pacific by a commanding 10 points and the Sharks were now in second place. However, Joe Thornton, their veteran star center, had injured his right knee two weeks ago and he wasn't playing Thursday at the SAP Center. In fact, nobody knew if "Jumbo Joe" would play again this season.

David Prior, the Golden Knights' goaltending coach, was probably thinking it might be a good idea to give Fleury the night off given the emotional experience he had 48 hours before. But Malcolm Subban hurt his hand during the morning skate and he would not be available. There was no time to recall one of the goalies from the AHL, so Fleury would get the start.

Subban, meanwhile, would dress but would not do anything other than skate around in the warmups. When the game started, his spot was not on the bench, given there is no room for the backup goalie to sit. Instead, he sat by the tunnel leading to the ice where he could watch with the fans in close proximity. Or he could choose to watch from a television monitor set up near the gate.

The Sharks had struggled to contain the Knights' overall speed in their first meeting, and it was the same case again as Haula, Karlsson and Neal all scored in what would be a 5-3 Vegas victory, ending the trip on a positive note. Fleury had 35 saves in the win and it helped take some of the sting out of losing to the Penguins two nights earlier.

The Knights went 4-2 on the trip, despite the fact they were without several regulars including Carrier, Sbisa, Nosek and now Subban. But the team's depth was proving to be productive, and Ryan Carpenter, Brad Hunt, Oscar Lindberg and Brendan Leipsic were finding ways to get the job done.

This was supposed to be one of the litmus tests for the first-year team and they had passed it.

"We had some struggles, but at the end we found a way to win, and that's awesome," said Marchessault. "Any win in the West is a big game, and teams are going to come ready to play us. To get four wins, especially on the road against good teams, that's big."

Having survived the longest and most arduous road trip of the year, the Golden Knights were going to get the opportunity to make more history and take a major step toward securing a postseason berth in their inaugural season.

They were 36-14-4. Twenty-eight games remained. The next seven were at T-Mobile Arena where they were a remarkable 19-4-1 so far. They were managing their injuries and the top players were producing with career seasons.

There was still a handful of teams the Knights had yet to meet and the Philadelphia Flyers were one of them. The Flyers were an interesting mix, with a bunch of youngsters thrown in with some young veterans. Their future appeared bright and they were in a battle within the Metropolitan Division to make the playoffs. They weren't going to be pushovers.

Brayden McNabb got the Knights off to a good start by scoring the game's first goal midway through the first period. But the Flyers tied it late in the first period, then went ahead 2-1 late in the second as Andrew MacDonald scored only his third goal of the season. The Flyers had managed just 14 shots in 40 minutes against Fleury but had two of them go in.

Fleury figured to get the bulk of the work as Malcolm Subban tended to his injured hand. Maxine Lagace, who had been playing well in the AHL, was recalled from the Chicago Wolves to serve as Fleury's understudy. He saw it as a great opportunity to learn from a future Hall of Famer.

"He's amazing," Lagace said of Fleury. "He's a real pro. He has such a great attitude. He's working hard, but he's also having fun. I just want to take everything in and learn as much as I can."

The Knights thought they were in good shape, down just 2-1 entering the third period. But they couldn't get the puck by Michal Neuvirth in the Philadelphia net. Neuvirth made 38 saves and the Flyers went on to a 4-1 win. It seemed eerily reminiscent of the start of the December homestand when unheralded Carolina came into T-Mobile and left with a win. Not that the Flyers were a bad team, but this was a game the Knights expected to put in the left-hand column.

They would right the ship two nights later, beating Chicago 5-2. The Blackhawks were still without goaltender Corey Crawford, and they were still languishing at the bottom of the Central Division. Tomas Nosek had returned to the Knights' lineup after missing a month with an upper-body injury and he scored into an empty net with 1:16 to play for the final goal. It was a nice way for Nosek to return as he found himself back with Pierre-Edouard Bellemare along with Ryan Carpenter, who was taking Will Carrier's place on the fourth line. Carpenter had also scored the team's first goal to tie the game 1-1 five minutes in.

The organization was unable to enjoy the win as it had received news that amateur scout Mark Workman had died after a brief battle with cancer. Workman took ill in October, was found to have liver cancer in late December and was dead by mid-February. He was just 47 years old.

"He had a keen eye for talent, a great sense of player evaluation and simply loved the game of hockey," General Manager George McPhee said of Workman, who had been hired in 2016 after spending 21 years coaching and working in college hockey. "We were all privileged to work with Mark and call him a friend."

On the ice, the Knights followed up the win over Chicago by beating Edmonton 4-1 for the first time in three tries and dominating the Oilers. Carpenter scored for the second straight game and it was his fourth of the season. William Karlsson also scored and it was a milestone goal, his 30th of the year, which was an unthinkable number given his status back in training camp when he played on the fourth line.

"It's pretty good," Karlsson said of his achievement. "Like I said, I didn't think I'd be here scoring that many goals before the season. But here I am, and I just want to continue doing that."

Coach Gerard Gallant wasn't impressed. Actually, he was, when he said kiddingly: "He better have 40 when it's all said and done."

It was a fun evening all the way around. A couple got married after Golden Knights fan Steve Poscente proposed to his girlfriend Cari Ivey during the first period. There was nothing unusual about that. You see marriage proposals all the time at sporting events.

But what made this one unique was Poscente and Ivey were going to be wed that night, in T-Mobile Arena, between the second and third periods. An Elvis impersonator performed the ceremony in front of 18,030 witnesses, and the couple danced their first dance to The King's "Can't Help Falling In Love" as the fans cheered.

After the game, Gallant was told of the wedding and was asked if he had a problem if one of his players tied the knot during a Golden Knights game.

"As long as they're not playing," he said with a chuckle.

The Knights were in a nice rhythm. Play one day, get the next one off, then play another game. They were facing Montreal next, and they weren't dealing with Charlie Lindgren this time, as had been the case back in November. Carey Price was back in goal but the Canadiens were still struggling. Yet they were hell-bent on making a statement on this Saturday. As is the case on any Saturday when the Canadiens were playing, the game was televised nationally on Hockey Night In Canada, and the Habs didn't want to be embarrassed on national TV.

But the Knights' momentum proved to be too much. They scored early and often and would go on to post a 6-3 win as Carpenter kept a hot hand with his third goal in as many games, while Reilly Smith scored twice to give him 19 goals for the season. Price gave way in the third period to Antti Niemi, and Fleury stopped 30 of the 33 shots he would face.

The one negative was Bellemare, who was injured in the first period and did not return. He had hurt his hand and would miss a couple of weeks, completing the trifecta of injuries to his line. Carrier was still out. Nosek had missed nearly a month. Now it was Bellemare's turn to sit out. And while one might say, "It's only the fourth line, what's the big deal?" The reality was that the fourth line had sustained the team all season and was an important part of Gallant's strategy. He liked rolling out four lines, not only for the sake of continuity but to save some legs and have his top lines ready to compete in the late stages of games.

With Bellemare out and James Neal suffering from an intestinal virus, the Knights called up Tomas Hyka and Stefan Matteau from Chicago. Hyka had played well in training camp but got caught in a numbers game and started the season in the minors. But he was fast, had a good shot and he could fit in anywhere. Matteau was strong and steady on his skates. His father, Stephane, was remembered for scoring a huge goal in the New York Rangers' Stanley Cup run in 1994 when he beat the New Jersey Devils in the second overtime in Game 7 of the Eastern Conference Finals. The two new Knights would be in the lineup when the team faced Anaheim on February 19.

It was a defensive battle, but Jakob Silfverberg's goal 13:32 in the first period would be all Anaheim would need. The Ducks did a great job clogging the neutral zone, taking away the Knights' speed and forcing them to the perimeter. They limited Vegas' quality scoring chances, and John Gibson and Ryan Miller combined on what would be a 2-0 shutout, the first combined shutout by the team since 2001. Gibson had injured his leg after a collision with Reilly Smith behind the Anaheim net late in the second period and gave way to Miller, who kept the door shut the final 20 minutes, thanks to a stout defense. It was a big win for the Ducks, who were trying to solidify their own postseason fortunes.

The Knights still had a winning ledger for the seven-game homestead. They were 3-2 with two games remaining, one with Calgary, the other against Vancouver. Neal was still recovering from the flu as the Knights hosted the Flames. It wasn't until late in the second period when Alex Tuch scored that Vegas could wrest control of the contest against the feisty Flames, who were not rolling over despite playing backup David Rittich in goal.

But the Knights had too much firepower. Luca Sbisa was back after his hand injury and he delivered 3:17 into the third period to make it 5-3. The Knights finished off the Flames on goals from Haula and Cody Eakin for a 7-3 win.

Two nights later, they completed the seven-game homestead with a 6-3 win over the Canucks. Hyka scored his first NHL goal to open the scoring just 2:29 into the game, only to see Vancouver rally to take a 2-1 lead.

The Knights came back with a pair of goals from Karlsson followed by a power-play goal from Marchessault. Suddenly it was 4-2 and Nosek made it 5-2 late in the second period. They chased yet another opposing goaltender from the game as starter Anders Nilsson gave way to Jacob Markstrom at the beginning of the third period.

It was a great way to end the homestead as Vegas finished 5-2 and remained firmly entrenched at the top of the Pacific Division. But the NHL trade deadline was looming and McPhee was already making moves. He got the Knights involved in a complicated three-way deal with Pittsburgh and

Ottawa that brought the Knights rugged forward Ryan Reaves and a fourth-round draft pick for 2018.

With Carrier still out and no timetable for his return, the Knights needed some toughness up front. Reaves, an eight-year NHL veteran who had played with David Perron in St. Louis, and was well-liked in the locker room, was the answer.

Before the season, the speculation was that Perron and Neal, both of whom were going to be unrestricted free agents at the end of the year, would be moved by the trade deadline. Of course, no one was expecting the Knights to be a first-place team and on their way to the playoffs back then. And both Neal and Perron were critical elements to the team's success to date.

The question McPhee was pondering was whether this team was good enough, as constructed, to challenge for the Stanley Cup? Barring a collapse of epic proportions, the Knights appeared to be headed to the playoffs, even though six weeks remained on the regular-season schedule. Was he willing to make a major deal and possibly break up the chemistry in the locker room he had worked so hard to assemble and develop?

The Knights were in Los Angeles the morning of February 26 to face the Kings. The trade deadline was at noon Pacific time. McPhee was working the phones, listening to offers and deliberating whether or not to do anything.

Mid-morning he made one move, sending Brendan Leipsic to Vancouver for defenseman Philip Holm. But behind the scenes, a major move was developing.

Ottawa and its all-star defenseman Erik Karlsson were at loggerheads over his future. Karlsson was going to be a UFA in 2019 and the Senators wanted to sign him to an extension. But Karlsson, who was making $6.5 million for the next two years, would not accept a home-team discount. He was looking for big money that was befitting his status as one of the game's premier players.

Senators general manager Pierre Dorion was in a tough spot. He had an unhappy player on his hands who happened to be his best player. His fan base, already agitated by the way the season had unfolded, was demanding change. Owner Eugene Melnyk, who was trying to get a new arena built downtown and was meeting resistance from the local and provincial governments, was digging in his heels. He wasn't about to pay anyone eight figures, and it only added to the dysfunction of the franchise.

Erik Karlsson would be a major upgrade to the Golden Knights. He might be the one to put things over the top and make the team a legitimate Stanley Cup contender. After all, Karlsson had guided Ottawa to the conference finals the year before, all the while playing with a broken ankle. Imagine what a healthy Karlsson could do?

The Senators were willing to part with their captain. But they wanted a lot in return. In addition to Karlsson, Ottawa wanted McPhee to take Bobby Ryan, the high-priced forward who was making $7.25 million and whose contract ran through 2022. They also wanted some draft picks and at least one prospect, preferably Cody Glass, who the Knights had selected last June with the No. 6 overall pick. They weren't interested in Neal or Perron. After all, Ottawa was looking to cut salary, not add to it.

The deadline was rapidly approaching. McPhee conferred with his hockey staff. He had always been successful building his teams through the draft, and while the Knights had space under the salary cap to accommodate both Karlsson and Ryan, the long-term ramifications, particularly in Ryan's case, made it seem counter-productive. In addition, there was no guarantee Karlsson would agree to an extension, and McPhee didn't believe in rental players, even if they were elite.

As he was contemplating what to do, Ken Holland, the Detroit Red Wings' GM, was calling. Would the Knights be interested in doing something to acquire forward Tomas Tatar, who had been a 20-goal scorer through most of his career? Tatar was only 27, and despite making $5.3 million, would be locked up for the next three-plus years.

The asking price from Detroit? Draft picks, something McPhee had a surplus of. One of the picks the Red Wings wanted was a first-rounder, and with the Knights' trending upward in the standings, their first-round pick for 2018 was falling lower and lower. Still, it was the only first-round pick the team had, and McPhee had to weigh that against acquiring a proven scorer.Tatar had 16 goals at the deadline and he was healthy. And yes, the Knights could use some additional scoring.

McPhee told Holland he'd get back to him. He got Dorion on the phone and asked him to go through the Karlsson-Ryan deal one more time. He listened and told Dorion, "No thanks." Perhaps down the road they could revisit a Karlsson trade. Meanwhile, he reached back to Holland. Could the Red Wings live without a first-round pick to get the deal done?

Holland insisted on a first-rounder. And with about 15 minutes to go before the deadline, McPhee agreed. The Knights would get Tatar. In return, Detroit would get Vegas' first-round draft pick for 2018, a second-round pick in 2019 and a third-rounder in 2021.

The backlash was swift. Fans decried the move and the media questioned McPhee's motive. Trade away a first-rounder for a guy with a minus-8 in the NHL's plus-minus rating who was underachieving?

People weren't too thrilled with the Reaves deal either, believing it would disrupt the chemistry in the locker room.

McPhee responded to the criticism by saying: "It's the one area where we're deep — we have a lot of picks. We spread it over four years. There are times when the decisions you make are all data driven and there are times when it's market driven. That was the price. We either get the player we thought we needed to have and give up those assets, or you don't. And I wanted to help the club."

It wouldn't take long to tell whether McPhee had helped or hurt the club.

15. Final Push For The Postseason

Ryan Reaves was in the lineup at Staples Center as the new-look Knights faced the Los Angeles Kings. So was James Neal, who was feeling better and had put the intestinal virus that had shelved him for two games behind him. Tomas Tatar was en route from Detroit and he would join his new team in Las Vegas in time for Tuesday's back end of the home-and-home series with the Kings.

Coach Gerard Gallant downplayed the changes, saying he was glad to have anyone who could help the team on his roster. And against the Kings, it never hurt to have some additional muscle. The rivalry between the two franchises was heating up. The Kings didn't care for the upstart expansion team and the feeling was mutual. There was bad blood, and it would get worse.

Kyle Clifford, the Kings' fourth-line forward and a tough guy in his own right, elbowed Oscar Lindberg in the head as Lindberg was trying to get back to the bench less than two minutes into the game. It was a cheap shot and no penalty was called on the play. Lindberg, who was knocked woozy from the hit, headed right to the locker room for concussion protocol. He would not return for weeks.

Reaves was on the ice at the time of the hit and he went after Clifford, only to have the linesmen intercede and temporarily keep the peace. But once again, the Knights were going to be without a player, and it disrupted the flow of playing four lines. Gallant would have to shuffle his lineup.

Erik Haula got the Knights on the board first, beating Jonathan Quick 4:37 in as Neal set him up in front. But Neal took a hard hit behind the net in the second period and appeared to have hurt his hand or wrist. He would not return. Now the Knights were down to 10 forwards, and Gallant was forced to essentially go with three lines. There was also a parade to the penalty box which wasn't helping matters.

It stayed that way until the first minute of the third period when Reilly Smith made it 2-0. Could the Knights find a way to hold the lead?

Jeff Carter had just returned to the LA lineup after missing most of the season with an Achilles tendon injury he suffered in October. He got his first goal of the season as he beat Marc-Andre Fleury with 7 1/2 minutes to play to cut the lead to 2-1.

The goal energized the majority of the 18,230 inside the Staples Center and the Kings fed off the energy of their crowd. The hitting on the ice intensified and tempers were running short. After every whistle there seemed to be a scrum as players from both teams got together, pushing and shoving each other and getting their sticks up in each other's faces.

Still, the Knights held the lead and, when Quick was pulled for an extra attacker, the Kings looked for the equalizer. They got it when Anze Kopitar, their leading scorer, was left alone inside the right face-off circle and his deadly accurate shot eluded Fleury with 11 seconds remaining. The goal sent the crowd into a frenzy and the Staples Center shook as if an earthquake had hit it.

The game would go to overtime and while the Knights were disappointed, they still were going to come out of it with at least one point. And they did it playing with just 10 forwards. But they put themselves in a tough spot as Colin Miller was called for hooking 2:34 into the five-minute extra period. Forty seconds into the penalty, the Kings won it as Dustin Brown knocked home the rebound of Tyler Toffoli's shot for a 3-2 victory.

"I'm not disappointed at all. I thought we played great," Gallant said. "The first goal goes off our guy's face and in the net and they made a great play to tie it up 2-2. It was a big point for us and they got two."

Gallant's bigger concern was Clifford's hit on Lindberg.

"I didn't like it," Gallant said of the play. "I didn't think it was a good hit. When a guy gets hurt, I don't like it."

With the events of Monday fresh in their minds, the Knights flew home and prepared for Tuesday's rematch with the Kings at T-Mobile Arena. Tatar would be in the lineup, but Neal and Lindberg would not.

Reaves would also be on the ice and he would be the point man on any revenge his new team might be seeking. But at the start the Knights appeared to be focused on winning as Karlsson scored 5:27 into the contest against backup goalie Jack Campbell for an early 1-0 lead. The Knights were also looking to play physical, which really wasn't their style. Perron took a roughing penalty midway through the first period and Reaves would take a roughing and a boarding penalty in a four-minute span. Gallant wasn't happy about the way the calls were going, and he let referees Dan O'Hallaran and Garrett Rank know about it. The team got a bench minor for arguing too vociferously and the Kings, who had rallied to take a 3-1 lead late in the second period, finished off the Knights as Carter scored on a power play with 1:58 remaining.

Not only did the Knights lose the game, they lost another player to injury — as Sbisa was hurt in the third period and did not return. It would be his third trip to the injured-reserve list.

Nate Schmidt was also banged up and the defenseman was going to take a few days off to heal and rejuvenate. In addition, Deryk Engelland was also in need of a little time off as well, and Gallant kept his practices short. He allowed his veterans to bypass the game-day morning skates. He had been trying to save his players' legs all season and now, with the injuries mounting and everyone sore, Gallant leaned on his depth to get through the next couple of weeks.

"Nobody's feeling sorry for us," Gallant said. "Injuries are part of the game. Every team goes through it and you manage them the best you can."

After losing 5-4 at home to Ottawa on March 2, the Knights were back on the road for five games, beginning in Newark, New Jersey, against the Devils. It was the final extended trip on the schedule and a successful run would all but lock up a playoff berth.

Fleury had been getting all the work and he showed no signs of fatigue. He was doing his job and giving his team a chance to win every night. That was the case in the 3-2 win over the Devils as Tatar scored what would be the game-winner on a power play late in the second period for his first goal as a member of the Knights.

Two nights later, the team was in Columbus to face the Blue Jackets. Things didn't start so well as Artemi Panarin scored just 16 seconds into the match, setting off the ubiquitous Civil War cannon that was fired inside Nationwide Arena every time the Jackets scored. It was quite disconcerting to hear, especially if you weren't accustomed to the big boom.

Haula tied the game 1:30 into the second period as the team had settled down and caught a break when a second Columbus goal had been nullified after Gallant challenged the play for being offsides. Tommy Cruz, the team's video coach, was in charge of eyeing infractions. He had worked for Gallant in Florida and was brought to Vegas after Gallant had taken the Knights' job. Cruz quickly relayed the information to the bench and recommended whether or not to challenge goaltender interference of offsides.

He was really good at spotting an offsides infraction but didn't have as much success when it came to goalie interference. That wasn't necessarily Cruz's fault because nobody in the NHL seemed to know what truly was goalie interference. Even the most clear-cut cases seemed open to interpretation.

But Cruz was a valued member of the coaching staff, and he helped keep the Knights in this one. However, Columbus scored twice in the second period to break the deadlock and take a 3-1 lead into the third period. And with Joonas Korpisalo standing on his head in the Blue Jackets' net and frustrating the Knights' forwards, there was no coming back. The final score was 4-1 and Korpisalo, who had stopped 37 of the 38 shots he faced, was selected as the game's No. 1 star.

But the toughest part of the loss was losing Reilly Smith to an upper-body injury after he took a hard check into the boards from David Savard in the second period. He was hunched over in pain when he skated back to the bench. His left arm or wrist appeared to be the issue and it looked to be serious.

Smith was playing really well. He had 22 goals and 38 assists and was a key member of the team's top line. Nobody knew how long he would be out.

It was on to Detroit and a reunion for Tatar, who was spending the day before the game with the Red Wings packing up his apartment and gathering his belongings. He had no time to do so after the trade the week before so he took advantage of the day off.

It was also the first visit to Little Caesars Arena, the Red Wings' spectacular new home which seated 20,000 and was a huge upgrade over Joe Louis Arena, the team's previous rink. It was a great place to watch hockey although it wasn't so super for playing hockey. The ice had been criticized by home and visiting players alike, and though it wasn't quite as bad as the Barclays Center in Brooklyn, it wasn't close to being as good as the ice had been at "The Joe".

The fact the arena had been booked for the Horizon League college basketball tournament a couple of days before didn't help matters, as the puck was bouncing and skittering and players struggled to hold an edge with their skate blades.

The Knights seemed to handle it, however. Alex Tuch scored 2:24 in and Cody Eakin scored twice in the second period to give the team a 3-0 lead. Tuch finished the scoring with his second of the game and 13th of his rookie season as the Knights bounced back with an impressive 4-0 win. Fleury stopped all 28 shots he faced and recorded his third shutout of the season.

Buffalo was the next stop, and it was a homecoming of sorts for Tuch. He had grown up a Sabres fan while living outside of Syracuse, and he had over 150 family and friends coming to the game. Tuch picked up the tab for only a few select family members. Fortunately, the others were able to get into the building as the Sabres weren't exactly a hot ticket. They were one of the worst teams in the NHL, and their fans were already focusing on football and the Bills.

But the Sabres players hadn't given up. At least not on this Saturday afternoon. After 40 scoreless minutes, Justin Bailey beat Fleury off an odd-man rush to put Buffalo on the board, 1-0. It stayed that way until Engelland tied it with 4:14 to play. The game went to overtime with both teams squandering great chances to win it. Eventually, it was decided in a shootout, and Haula was the hero as he put the puck past Robin Lehner to give the Knights a 2-1 win.

The New York State High School Hockey Championships were being held in Buffalo at the Sabres' practice facility, which was attached to a hotel. The Knights were staying at the hotel. Fleury noticed the high schoolers roaming the halls and saw photos attached to the door next to his room. He became curious. So he knocked on the door and the players from Victor High School were shocked to see the Knights goaltender.

Fleury and the players chatted for a few minutes. He signed a few autographs and posed for selfies with some of them, and then he was gone.

"Going into the tournament there were rumors that the Golden Knights would be staying at the hotel, and it got us excited, and we were all looking around," Connor Gelabert, a junior defenseman told the Rochester Democrat & Chronicle. "Then there's a knock on the door and Marc-Andre Fleury is standing right there. Everyone in my room was kind of shocked because we didn't know what to do or say. But he knocked and introduced himself and asked about our tournament and how we were doing. We just kind of talked to him for a bit. It was crazy."

It was just another example of Fleury being Fleury.

The trip was already a success as the Knights flew to Philadelphia for Monday's match with the Flyers. Nate Schmidt had rejoined the team in Buffalo and his presence was big. The Flyers were very much in the playoff hunt, and to beat them would take everyone's best effort.

The teams traded goals over the first 47 minutes, and it was 2-2 with less than three minutes to play. But Carpenter took a pass from Eakin and beat Petr Mrazek for the game winner with 2:40 to go. Fleury turned aside 38 of the 40 shots he faced and the Knights ended the trip 4-1 after the 3-2 victory. They were now 45-19-5, and with 13 games left, 50 wins and 100 points were a very realistic possibility. They were already the best expansion team in sports history. The question now was, how great would they ultimately be?

As the Golden Knights entered the homestretch of their inaugural season, they were still in denial about the playoffs. At least the coach and his players were.

Gerard Gallant refused to acknowledge that his team was going to be playing meaningful hockey games in mid-April. His players weren't taking the bait either. They stuck to the script, the "one game at a time" mantra they had been following all year.

But the real goal for the Knights was to get healthy. They were still a banged up bunch and were missing key pieces. Up front, Reilly Smith and Will Carrier were still out. So was defenseman Luca Sbisa and goaltender Malcolm Subban. So with 13 games left, it was all about healing up.

Things didn't start well as the Knights were beaten at home by New Jersey 8-2 and by Minnesota 4-2 as the Wild swept the three games between the teams. Jason Zucker, who learned the game growing up in Las Vegas, scored during his first game in his hometown.

It was also his 29th goal of the year. Zucker would go on to score a career-best 33 goals and with his contract up at the end of the season, he figured to be in line for a nice payday. But the Wild would be eliminated in the first round of the playoffs, general manager Chuck Fletcher would be fired, and Zucker's future in St. Paul was very much up in the air. Zucker's older brothers, Evan and Adam, were involved with the Junior Golden Knights youth hockey program, and they were working to grow interest in the game in Las Vegas.

The last things the Knights needed at this point were more injuries and more losses. They got some good news as Subban was ready to play and he dressed for the March 18 game against Calgary. Fleury remained in the Vegas net and he was given more than enough support as Karlsson notched the second hat trick of his career in a 4-0 shutout at T-Mobile Arena.

Karlsson now had an unbelievable 39 goals and even he was starting to believe that he was doing great things. Maybe he could get to 50? He certainly seemed a lock to reach the 40-goal plateau.

Two nights later, the Knights had a huge scare. Fleury took a puck off his mask, courtesy of a slap shot from Brandon Sutter, and did not return for the second period. Given his history of concussions, he was headed to concussion protocol, and nobody was saying what the extent of his condition was.

Subban was thrust into action and he came into the game with a 3-0 lead, thanks to first-period goals from Jonathan Marchessault, Cody Eakin and Pierre-Edouard Bellemare. Tomas Tatar scored with 5:39 left in the second period to make it 4-0 and Subban stopped all but one of the 23 shots he faced in what would be a 4-1 Vegas victory.

"As soon as we realized Subban was going in, we talked to each other in the locker room and said, let's make sure we're strong in front of him," Bellemare said. "Subban hasn't played in a while and he needed us to play a strong defensive game in front of him."

But the big concern was Fleury. Was he going to be out for another long stretch? Would he be available for the playoffs?

Fleury did not make the trip to San Jose for the March 22 game against the Sharks. Oscar Dansk, who had recovered from his knee injury, was to serve as Subban's backup. Subban was fine and he had an early 1-0 lead as Tatar had scored 3:47 into the contest. But Brent Burns tied it for the Sharks early in the second period and in overtime, Logan Couture won it 2-1 at 39 seconds after the Knights failed to cash in at the other end against Martin Jones.

The Knights were headed to Denver, and Fleury met the team there. He had passed all the neurological tests and he kidded reporters saying he was able to catch up on watching "Days Of Our Lives," his favorite soap opera.

The city of Las Vegas breathed a sigh of relief. Fleury was in goal against the Avalanche at the Pepsi Center on March 24, and he showed no ill effects from the shot off the mask. But he received little offensive support as the Knights were chasing the game for the final 45 minutes until Marchessault scored with 1:15 left and sent the game to overtime. It went to a shootout and Gabriel Landeskog won it for the Avs, 2-1.

Still, Vegas got a point out of it. And with the final homestand of the season coming up, the Knights were closing in on clinching the Pacific Division title.They started with a 4-1 win over Colorado to gain a split of the back-to-back meetings with the Avalanche. But two nights later the woeful Coyotes got a pair of goals from Kevin Connauton, including the eventual game-winner, and Arizona finally beat the Knights in their final meeting 3-2.

The last two games were on Friday against St. Louis and Saturday against San Jose. If things broke right against the Blues, the Knights would clinch a tie for the division. They did their part, winning 4-3 on Marchessault's overtime goal 20 seconds in. Marchessault, who had also scored in the first period, now had 27 goals for the season. He was three shy of equalling his career-high of 30 from the year before with Florida. Karlsson also scored, giving him 41 for the year while Neal notched his 25th goal.

The next night, the memories of opening night came flooding back as the team prepared to play its final home game of the regular season. A video tribute was played, and a black and gold banner with the names of the 58 shooting victims of October 1 and the words "VEGAS STRONG" was hoisted to the rafters. The team also announced it was retiring the number 58 in honor of the victims. Nobody had worn it and nobody ever would.

The crowd was fired up, and the fans saw a heck of a game. The teams traded goals over the first two periods and it was 2-2 heading toward the midway point of the third period. Jon Merrill was in the penalty box for tripping, and it was a critical kill for the Knights. Gallant sent Karlsson over the boards, and seconds later, perhaps the most magical play of the season occurred.

Burns was at the point for San Jose, looking to pinch and keep the puck in the Knights' zone. But Karlsson and his high hockey IQ read the play. He reached out and deflected the puck before Burns could get it. Karlsson then skated past the San Jose all-star defenseman and broke in alone on goaltender Martin Jones. Karlsson faked going to his backhand and got Jones to move. And as Jones tried to poke-check the puck away with his stick, Karlsson then went between his legs and lifted the puck over Jones' shoulder and into the net.

The crowd of 18,458 went nuts. The video board above center ice replayed the goal several times. Karlsson looked up and didn't say anything while his teammates tapped him on his shoulder and helmet to acknowledge the greatness they had just witnessed.

"I've done it before," Karlsson said matter-of-factly about his 42nd goal of the year. "I think I was 18 the last time I tried it. I don't think (Jones) was expecting it."

It was one of the top candidates for the NHL's Goal of the Year and people were trying to come up with one that was better.

Marchessault said: "It's a scoring chance, and if you miss the puck, you look a little stupid. It's a great play. But it's a highlight we're going to see for many years. He went with his gut. It was amazing."

But there was still plenty of time for the Sharks to mount a comeback. However, the Knights' defense was stellar in front of Fleury and he was up to the task as the Knights clinched the division title with a 3-2 win. They had 50 wins and 107 points, simply phenomenal numbers. According to the Elias Sports Bureau, the Knights were the first modern-era expansion team from any of the four North American professional sports leagues to win its division in its inaugural season. They were an amazing 29-10-2 at T-Mobile Arena.

"It's a great feeling to win our division," Gallant said. "Obviously, nobody had those expectations at the first of the season, but as we know, our team grew on everybody, and we played hard and we worked hard all season long. It's a great accomplishment, but we all know what the real accomplishment would be. It's all about the playoffs."

The team was on the road for three games to close out the regular season. Reilly Smith was on the trip, which started in Vancouver April 3. But he wasn't quite ready. Instead, veteran Brandon Pirri had been called up from the AHL's Chicago Wolves and was in the lineup as Gallant opted to rest Haula and Marchessault. David Perron was also out. He had injured his neck the week before against Colorado.

Pirri had been in the NHL with Florida and the Rangers and he would score twice in helping the Knights defeat the Canucks 5-4 in a shootout as Shea Theodore scored the game-winner in the fourth round. Karlsson scored the 43rd goal of his amazing season and Subban turned aside 21 shots for the win, Vegas' 51st.

It would be the final win of the regular season. It would also be the final time the Knights would face the Sedin twins, Daniel and Henrik. The twins had been mainstays in Vancouver their entire careers. Now, they were preparing to exit the stage, and following the game, the Knights players lined up to shake hands with the Sedins, a very classy gesture.

The Knights moved on to Edmonton and Smith would be held out one more game. Pirri stayed in the lineup and scored 4:47 into the second period to give the Knights a 2-1 lead. Subban, who was starting for the second straight game, was unable to close the door as the Oilers scored three unanswered third-period goals and beat the Knights 4-3.

It was the NHL debut for Zach Whitecloud, a defenseman from Bemidji State University who the Knights had signed in March as a collegiate free agent, their first-ever such signing. He had skated with the team for more than three weeks and with the Knights' playoff quest already fulfilled the decision was made to let Whitecloud get a taste of the big time.

"We want to see the kid play," Gallant said of Whitecloud, who took Nate Schmidt's place in the lineup and was paired with Brayden McNabb. "He's been with us for a while now and he knows what we're all about, so it's time to get him in there."

The regular-season finale was in Calgary and the team had a light practice Friday afternoon at the Scotiabank Saddledome. Shortly after the team returned to its downtown hotel, news broke out of Saskatchewan. A junior hockey team's bus had collided with a truck and there were multiple casualties and injuries.

The team, the Humboldt Broncos, was headed for a playoff game. There wasn't a single Golden Knights player, coach or executive who hadn't ridden a bus at some point to play in a game.

As the reports came out of Saskatchewan, the news worsened. First, it was reported that 12 people had died. Then the number climbed to 15. Eventually it would rise to 16. The other passengers were injured and were rushed to hospitals in Regina, the provincial capital and Saskatchewan's largest city.

The next morning both teams held their routine morning skates. But you could tell nobody's heart was in it. Glen Gulutzan, the Flames' coach, had ties to Saskatchewan. He was emotional as he talked, choking back tears.

"We're playing for the purity of the game, for the love of the game, because that's what those kids did," he said. "It's very, very tough what happened. I can't imagine what those families are going through. We've all ridden those buses during our careers and it puts things in perspective. I said in Winnipeg that our season is painful, and I would like to take that back."

Knights defenseman Brayden McNabb is from Saskatchewan. He understood the impact of what had happened to the Broncos better than most.

"My brother (Dean) is playing in Victoria," McNabb said. "But there was a chance he could have been there. It's scary thinking about it. But everyone in hockey rides the buses. You're riding through mountains and over flat roads. It's crazy thinking about it. My heart goes out to the families and the community. It's just a tough day."

Defenseman Brad Hunt said: "Everyone in here has rode the bus. You don't expect anything like that to happen or want to see anything like that happen. You're sitting on the bus with your buddies. Those guys are your brothers in junior hockey. It's just horrible news."

The Flames quickly put together a pregame ceremony to honor the Broncos. Both teams abandoned their usual place on their respective blue lines and stood together in solidarity at center ice. The Knights were no strangers when it came to these situations, and they joined the Flames as fans yelled, "Let's Go Broncos!" following a moment of silence.

Kelly McCrimmon, the Knights' assistant general manager, was in the Saddledome. The Humboldt tragedy had to have brought back memories of his brother Brad, who was coaching in Russia and died in a plane crash en route to a game in the Kontinental Hockey League back on September 7, 2011. If anyone could understand the grief the families of the Humboldt players and coaches were dealing with, it was McCrimmon.

It was under these difficult circumstances that the two teams were asked to entertain 19,289 people who had paid good money to take their minds off the news for a couple of hours.

The Knights had Reilly Smith back. On any other night, that would have been big news. But in light of the Humboldt tragedy, Smith's return took a back seat. He had been injured back on March 6 in Columbus and this was his first action since then. Smith had missed 15 games, and he had a lot of rust to shake off.

"The main focus was to get back up to the speed of play," Smith said. "There are parts of my game that I could see are still a little bit rusty, but it was good to get back out there."

The Flames were in control from the opening face-off. They weren't going to the playoffs. Gulutzan's future as head coach was very much up in the air. But as Gulutzan said, his team was playing for those kids from Humboldt.

Calgary had a 3-0 lead after 7 1/2 minutes and by the end of the second period it was 6-1 as Cody Eakin had managed to keep the Knights from being shut out with a goal 51 seconds into the period. Fleury was looking shaky for one of the rare times this season and Gallant took him out, putting Subban in the net for the start of the third period. No sense in risking an injury to his star goalie in what had become a meaningless game.

The final was 7-1, one of the Knights' worst losses of the year and certainly not the way a team with Stanley Cup aspirations wanted to go into the postseason.

"To get this game, you've got to be mentally prepared to play, and our guys didn't have much to play for and it really showed," Gallant said. "When you're not mentally prepared to play, that's what's going to happen."

But he was also philosophic about things. Fifty-one wins. One hundred nine points. A division title. All in the franchise's inaugural season. He really didn't have a whole lot to complain about.

"I'm disappointed right now," he said. "But believe me, it's been a great season and I'm not worried about it. It's going to have no effect on the game next Wednesday. We got through the game, nobody got hurt, and that's the key for us."

The playoffs were set. The Knights would face the Los Angeles Kings in the opening round. They couldn't have asked for a better opponent to get their attention as they would open the best-of-seven series at home. T-Mobile Arena was going to be rocking like never before.

16. The Quest Begins

It takes 16 victories to hoist the Stanley Cup. The Golden Knights were one of 16 teams which would have the opportunity to accomplish that feat.

There was a banner that hung in the team's offices, displaying games that numbered one through 15, with the Stanley Cup representing the 16th. Nobody knew how many numbers would get crossed off. But it served as a reminder to everyone in the organization that this was something everyone would play a role in.

It started with the fans. After seeing opposing teams pack T-Mobile Arena all season, the team decided it would try to limit access to visiting fans during the playoffs. Season-ticket members were asked to sign a pledge that they would not resell their tickets on the secondary market. It was called the "Knights Vow", and the majority of members signed on. In doing so, they received a 30 percent discount on the price of their tickets.

The team's practice sessions leading up to the opening of the first round were standing room only. Going back to Christmas, when kids were off from school and the Knights were starting to get everyone's attention, the stands at City National Arena were filling up. And why not? There was no admission charge to get in, parking was free and you could get a close-up look at the players, something that the majority of fans couldn't do on game night.

For the Knights' players and coaches, this was something they simply weren't used to. Virtually every team practiced in anonymity, with the doors closed and the only sounds you heard were those of skate blades cutting through the ice and pucks coming off sticks and either catching the boards or the glass. But here, it was the complete opposite. The fans would break into their "Go Knights Go!" chants before the first player, usually Pierre-Edouard Bellemare, hit the ice. Every player would receive a nice ovation as he entered the rink. But the loudest cheers would always be for Marc-Andre Fleury. Just the sight of No. 29 sent the fans into a frenzy, and he would usually acknowledge their love by raising his goalie stick.

Someone asked coach Gerard Gallant if having so many people watch his team practice was a distraction. "Not at all," he said. "I think it gives our guys an extra boost."

There were so many toddlers and young kids at the rink, decked out in Golden Knights jerseys, sweatshirts and hats, that it sometimes resembled hockey day care. They would press their little hands and faces up against the glass, and the players, seeing that, would acknowledge them with a little fist bump against the protective barrier in return.

The team had also set up an area for kids 14 and under to watch practice and to line up and get autographs afterward. It was the result of a few adult professional autograph-seekers who would camp out in front of the gate which led to the lot where the players parked their cars, and it had gotten so unwieldy that security was hired to maintain order. Eventually, everyone was banned from waiting outside and adults were no longer allowed to get autographs.

That did not sit well with some collectors, who had posters that the team gave away at every home game. Yes, there were some who were hoping to make a buck off the venture. But the majority merely loved their team and wanted a special keepsake from the inaugural season.

Still, the team didn't back down. The policy remained in place and that was that.

The Knights had gone 2-1-1 against the Kings in the regular season, and enough hate among the players and fans had developed over those four games to make their first-round matchup intriguing. The Knights still weren't 100 percent healthy. David Perron's neck was still bothering him. Luca Sbisa's hand was still not healed. Reilly Smith and Will Carrier were back, although both were trying to shake off the rust from their collective games.

But the team was ready to make its Cup run. Game 1 was set for April 11 and the Knights had home-ice advantage. So if the series was to go the full seven games, Game 7 would be at T-Mobile Arena.

The usual medieval pregame show was upgraded, and though the Golden Knight mascot still had a prominent role, it wasn't just pulling a sword out of a rock anymore. The goal of working the crowd into a frenzy was still in play, and Jonny Greco and his team pulled it off. They had added a couple of touches, including a huge Knights' helmet for the players to skate through as they entered the ice. It lit up and bellowed smoke, reminding you of the shark's head the San Jose team skated through in the SAP Center. An already loud building was somehow even louder, and Carnell Johnson hadn't even belted out the first note of The Star-Spangled Banner.

The Knights had been at their best when they scored first, particularly at home. And when Shea Theodore was able to skate in and beat Jonathan Quick just 3:23 into the game, it felt like the roof was going to come off T-Mobile Arena. Little did anyone realize at the time, but Theodore's goal would be the only one registered in Game 1.

Fleury was on his game, having shaken off the debacle in Calgary from a few days before. He was moving well, challenging the Los Angeles shooters, and his defense did a solid job of clearing any rebounds from in front and not giving the Kings' forwards any second chances.

Midway through the third period, Gallant threw his fourth line of Bellemare, Carrier and Nosek out on the ice. Carrier, who has deceptive speed, looked to get around Drew Doughty, the Kings' all-star defenseman. But Doughty caught Carrier up high in the head with his elbow, necessitating Carrier's departure from the game. And though Doughty did not receive a penalty for the hit, the NHL's Department of Player Safety determined that Doughty's hit was illegal and issued him a one-game suspension the following day.

The Kings tried to pull even, but Fleury was perfect, and the Knights were the 1-0 victors in Game 1. Fleury had stopped all 30 shots he faced. It was his 11th career playoff shutout, and his 63rd career victory in the postseason, which was tops among all active goaltenders. He had robbed Anze Kopitar and Dustin Brown in the third period to help keep his team in front.

"I felt good. My teammates were great also," Fleury said. "They helped me out a lot, blocking shots and keeping guys away from the front of the net. It makes my job a little easier."

It was a physical opener, with the teams combining for 132 hits. But it was Doughty's hit on Carrier that stood out. He would be suspended for Game 2, and the Kings, who were already down two defensemen — Jake Muzzin and Derek Forbort — would have to find a way to improvise.

It took the Knights a little longer to strike first in Game 2, but they ultimately took the lead as Alex Tuch scored on the power play 14:47 into the first period for a 1-0 lead. Once again, the Kings struggled to put the puck past Fleury, who picked up where he left off two nights before. But with just over four minutes left in the second period, Los Angeles finally scored when Paul Ladue, who was left alone in front, beat Fleury to tie the game 1-1.

The game went to overtime. Then a second extra sudden death period. With 4:38 left in what was the longest game in team history, Haula ended it, beating Quick from inside the right circle for a 2-1 win and a 2-0 lead in the series. Neal had drawn two Kings defenders to him as he skated into the Los Angeles zone and made a nifty pass to Haula, who had supported the puck.

Haula had wound up stuck on 29 goals through the final week of the regular season, never making it to 30. However, this was the biggest goal of his life.

"I was coming in with a lot of speed, and I was just trying to freeze him (Quick) for a little bit," Haula said. "I took what they gave me. I went by the d-man, and coming in alone, I was able to freeze him a little bit and slide it in five-hole. We knew they would be better and they were going to be desperate. We just stressed about playing the same way, the whole time. That has worked for us all season long, us using our speed, wearing teams down and putting a lot of pucks to the net and getting traffic in there. That's the thing that we stress, and that's the thing we're going to keep doing."

The series shifted to the Staples Center for Game 3, and both teams were changing things up. Drew Doughty was back after serving his one game suspension, which he called "a bunch of bull—", and coach John Stevens also welcomed back Muzzin to the Kings' blueline. Muzzin had a couple of Stanley Cup rings to his credit and perhaps his presence might help change the narrative.

The Knights were also shifting their lineup. Tomas Tatar had been ineffective in the first two games, and David Perron was ready. So Perron was in and Tatar was out. But Perron did not return to his regular line with Haula and Neal. Instead, he was on the third line with Cody Eakin and Ryan Carpenter while Alex Tuch stayed on the second line.

The Kings took their first lead in the series when Alex Iafallo scored 13:14 into Game 3. But Perron made his presence felt as he helped set up Eakin's game-tying goal 6:10 into the third period. The goal appeared to give the Knights the lift they were looking for, and they picked up the pace, using their superior speed to create opportunities in front of Quick. With 5 1/2 minutes left in regulation, Neal got his first goal of the playoffs to give Vegas a 2-1 lead. Twenty-one seconds later, William Karlsson scored his first playoff goal to make it 3-1.

The Kings were in big trouble. Unless they could rally, they would be looking at an 0-3 deficit, and their fate would virtually be sealed. With Quick off the ice for a sixth attacker and just over two minutes to play, Kopitar delivered and pulled his team to within a goal at 3-2. But Fleury and his defense closed the door and the Knights held on for the win and a commanding lead in the series.

"They've been great and it's been fun to watch," Fleury said of his defensemen. "Tonight wasn't easy. They scored first, we had a lot of penalties. Guys battled hard until the end again. They were coming, and the guys did a great job to get the puck out."

The Kings, obviously frustrated, weren't capitulating.

"We had a couple of chances in the second and third periods that maybe we should have buried, but they came back and scored on their chances," forward Adrian Kempe said. "It was tough. I think we did a pretty good game, but it's not enough. We've gotta get better."

Kopitar said: "Yeah, I mean, we're down but we're not out. So there's at least one game left to be played. We've gotta start with winning one and go from there."

Kopitar asked what it would take for the Kings to get back into the series?

"Play better, obviously," Kopitar said. "Tonight was better again, but not good enough."

The Knights were also saying all the right things, about how the last one is the toughest to win and all the other cliches. But with Fleury playing at such a high standard, the team with the lead wasn't about to gag. As Game 4 began, with a large number of fans making the trip from Las Vegas to hopefully watch their team clinch, the Knights stuck with their plan. They looked to attack whenever possible, though mindful of the fact that the Kings were an excellent counter-attacking team and could strike at any time.

After a scoreless first period, the Knights found offense from an unlikely source. Defenseman Brayden McNabb, the one-time King, was left alone at the point as the Kings were trying to contain Karlsson, Smith and Marchessault, who were doing good work keeping control in the Los Angeles zone. McNabb had just five goals in the regular season, and he wouldn't have been the first choice of most folks when it came to being a goal-scoring hero.

But McNabb had a good, if not underrated shot. He wasn't afraid to let it rip. So as Smith had the puck in the middle, McNabb saw nothing but open ice on the right side and filled the void. Smith, who has great peripheral vision, saw him out of the corner of his eye, and made a perfect pass which McNabb one-timed, a-la- Karlsson, past Quick.

The Knights fans in the crowd of 18,422 went nuts. The rest of the building fell deathly silent. They knew the way things had been going that this one-goal lead could just as well have been three or four. And given the way Fleury was playing in the Vegas net, it was going to be tough for the home team to stay alive. Never mind the 35-plus minutes which still had to be played.

Sure enough, Fleury made the 1-0 lead stand up. He turned away all 31 shots, including yet another big save on Dustin Brown, who had been robbed on at least two other occasions earlier in the series. Time had run out on the Kings, and as the Knights lined up for the traditional post-series handshakes, they did so with the knowledge they would be playing more hockey for at least another couple of weeks.

"Everybody contributes to our success," said Fleury, who had a 0.65 goals-against average and a .977 save percentage in the series. "We roll four lines, six D are playing, and I think that's what makes our strength. Everybody is contributing and adding to our success every night."

Gallant knew that with a different bounce or two, his team could have been on the wrong side of that handshake line.

"It has been incredible," Gallant said. "It's two good teams, and I guess basically we got a little bit more puck luck than they did, and we cashed in at the right times."

The Knights were going to have some time to rest and heal up. The San Jose Sharks were putting the finishing touches on sweeping the Anaheim Ducks, and they would be the Knights' second-round opponent. They would meet nine days from now in Las Vegas.

At the team's offices in City National Arena they had 'X'd' the first four numbers on the Stanley Cup scoreboard banner. More X's were coming.

17. Swimming With Sharks

The Golden Knights had swept their way into the second round of the Stanley Cup playoffs. But they knew that with a couple of bounces of the puck going the other way, it could have been a much different story.

Yet they were moving on. The San Jose Sharks had played the Knights tough during the regular season, and even with the status of veteran center Joe Thornton very much up in the air, Peter DeBoer's team was not going to be an easy out by any means.

Once again Vegas had home-ice advantage for the best-of-seven series, and the Knights were well-rested when Game 1 began on April 26 at T-Mobile Arena. The NHL mandated that no series could start until all first-round series had been concluded, and the Sharks, who had swept the Anaheim Ducks to advance, also found themselves sitting and waiting.

If there was any rust, it appeared to lie with the Sharks. They looked to be a bit slow getting out of the starting gate, and the Knights made them pay. Cody Eakin, who had a strong series in the first-round sweep of the Kings, got things going just 4:31 into the game for a 1-0 lead. Erik Haula, the hero of Game 2 vs. the Kings with his double-overtime game-winner, made it 2-0 only 26 seconds later. The lead grew to 3-0 as Jonathan Marchessault followed up Haula's goal by scoring

1:05. And after Alex Tuch scored on a power play to increase the lead to 4-0, DeBoer had seen enough. He yanked Martin Jones from the Sharks' net and inserted backup goaltender Aaron Dell.

By now, the sellout crowd of 18,444 was in full throat, imploring the Knights to finish off Game 1. Essentially, Tuch's goal had done just that.

Shea Theodore had scored in the second period to give Vegas a commanding 5-0 lead heading into the final 20 minutes. The Sharks were clearly frustrated at this point, and Evander Kane let his emotions get the best of him. Marc-Andre Fleury had stopped a shot with 3:25 gone in the third period, and there was the requisite scrum in front of him with Nate Schmidt and Joe Pavelski the main antagonists. Pierre-Edouard Bellemare was also nearby. Kane decided he would join the fray and he targeted Bellemare, cross-checking him in the face with his stick.

Bellemare went to the locker room for repairs. So did Kane, who had been assessed a game misconduct along with a five-minute major for cross-checking. He also could expect a call the next day from the NHL's Department of Player Safety.

The Knights cashed in twice on the power play, with Colin Miller and James Neal beating Dell. The final would be 7-0. Fleury had his third shutout in five playoff games and the Knights had established themselves early in the series.

As was the case with Drew Doughty's hit to Will Carrier's head in Game 1 of the first round, the NHL suspended Kane for one game for his hit on Bellemare. Like Doughty, Kane wasn't happy with the decision, but what could he do?

With Kane out for Game 2, there was growing speculation Thornton might play. His surgically repaired knee had healed to the point where he could practice. And with the Sharks down a game in the series as well as being down a key forward, might this not be the perfect time for "Jumbo Joe" to get in the lineup and give his team a lift?

Thornton was on the ice for the warmups for Game 2 on April 28. But he would not play. Instead, Barclay Goodrow would take Kane's spot. DeBoer also shuffled his lines a bit and got his team to play tighter defensively.

With just two minutes remaining in the first period, William Karlsson beat Jones to open the scoring. Unlike the March 31 meeting, when Karlsson scored the memorable between-the-legs goal against Jones, this was the more conventional one-timer as he took a feed from Miller and scored.

Karlsson made it 2-0 just 26 seconds into the second period as Reilly Smith found him alone in front and made a great pass that resulted in Karlsson getting his third goal of the playoffs. It appeared the Knights were now off and running and looking to take a 2-0 lead in the best-of-seven series, while protecting home ice in the process. But San Jose stayed focused on the task at hand.

Yes, the Sharks were now chasing the game somewhat, but if they could get the next goal, they could perhaps change the tenor of the game.

Brent Burns did the honors as the all-star defenseman ripped a shot past Fleury for San Jose's first goal of the series. It cut the Knights' lead to 2-1 just two minutes into the second period, while David Perron sat in the penalty box. The goal was a huge momentum changer as the Sharks began to pick up their pace of play and the Knights began to lose their cool. They began a parade to the penalty box, picking up five infractions and forcing coach Gerard Gallant to shuffle his lines due to losing a lot of the continuity from the penalties.

Logan Couture tied it at 2-2 midway through the second, and Burns made it 3-2 less than three minutes later as the Sharks had their first lead of the series. From the Knights' perspective, this was a temporary setback. They had rallied many times during the year and they were at home. Their crowd was still very much behind them, and if they could just stay out of the box, they could regain control of Game 2.

Gallant's players got the message. Miller took a high-sticking penalty midway through the third period, but the Knights killed it off. Moments after Miller returned from the box, Schmidt tied it 3-3 with a blast from the point after Haula had kept the play alive in the San Jose end. Both teams had chances to win it in regulation but it would go to overtime.

Unlike the regular season where overtime is a five-minute affair played 3 on 3, playoff overtime is sudden death. You play until there's a winner, and it's played with a full compliment of 5 against 5.

With just over three minutes remaining in the first OT, Marchessault appeared to have scored the game-winner, having put the puck past Jones. But the Sharks claimed goaltender interference, and the video replay showed Marchessault had made contact with Jones in getting to the front of the net before he collected the puck and scored. The goal was disallowed and the game continued.

"I saw (Jones) was in his crease and I was out of his crease," Marchessault said of the play. "He moves his blocker towards me so I think it's just a referee's decision at that point and it didn't go our way. It's a tough decision and I didn't really think anything. If it didn't go our way, I just wanted to catch my breath and get ready to go."

Gallant said of the play: "They are tough calls. We've seen them all year long and they're tough calls. It went against us tonight, and you move on."

The game continued. It went to a second overtime and the message from Gallant to his team remained, "Stay out of the box." But defenseman Jon Merrill didn't get the message. He was whistled for a hooking penalty 5:05 into what was now the fifth period. Merrill had played well in Luca Sbisa's spot and with Sbisa getting closer but not quite ready to return to the lineup, Merrill was on the third pairing with Miller.

The Sharks didn't waste any time taking advantage. Couture got the puck at the left circle from Kevin Labanc, and he got off his shot quickly. Fleury was unable to react in time and the Sharks had a 4-3 victory. They had tied the series at a game apiece and had taken home-ice advantage away from the Golden Knights.

Games 3 and 4 were in San Jose. Kane would be returning to the lineup and maybe, just maybe, Thornton would declare himself fit to play. It appeared the series had flipped in the Sharks' favor.

The crowd at SAP Center in San Jose was amped up. The team had come up with a quirky jab at the visitors — "Nighty Knight". It appeared on the rally towels and had been spelled out in the seats in the balcony. The Golden Knights players got a kick out of it when they had their morning skate. But nobody in white was smiling when Timo Meier scored seven minutes into the second period to give the Sharks a 1-0 lead.

The Knights answered a couple of minutes later as Miller scored on the power play to tie it 1-1. Marchessault, the victim of the goal called back in Game 2, got this one to count as he put the Knights ahead 2-1 just 3 1/2 minutes later on another Vegas power play. Then Reilly Smith made it 3-1 just 1:15 after Marchessault's goal, and all the momentum the Sharks had built was suddenly gone. Or at least temporarily.

Kane got a bit of revenge, however, scoring nearly eight minutes into the third period to cut the deficit to 3-2. Tomas Hertl, who had been a pain in the Knights side in Game 2, pulled the Sharks even 3-3 with 1:57 to go, forcing overtime for the second straight game. The crowd was back in it, and the winner would have a big advantage going into the pivotal Game 4.

Back and forth it went. Both teams had great chances, same as in Game 2. Once again, the Knights scored as Karlsson fired a wrist shot from inside the right circle over Jones' shoulder for the game-winner. This one would count as the Knights won 4-3 and took a 2-1 lead in the series.

Neal, who hit the post moments earlier, had taken a feed near center ice from Marchessault, who was back-checking in his own end. Karlsson skated alone down the right side, and Neal hit him in stride. It was his fourth goal of the postseason, and Karlsson continued to be the Sharks' nemesis.

"I think it's good for the morale," Karlsson said. "We showed great attitude. Again, they came back. It was tough, too, but we gave someone a chance to be an overtime hero."

Karlsson was that hero with his Game 3 winner.

Despite being down in the series, the Sharks seemed far from finished. They responded like champions with a 4-0 win in Game 4. It was easily San Jose's best performance in the series, as goals from Marcus Sorensen and Joonas Donskoi late in the first period sent the Sharks on their way. Hertl and

Pavelski added goals in the second and third periods respectively, to seal the win.

Once again, Gallant's players failed to heed his warning about staying out of the penalty box. And while the Sharks cashed in on only one of their four power play opportunities, the seven penalties taken by Vegas disrupted its continuity when it came time to roll out four lines, which Gallant prefers to do.

Now, it was a best-of-three series. And while the Knights had regained home-ice advantage thanks to their Game 3 victory, they had some work still to do if they were to keep their Stanley Cup hopes alive.

Gallant made a couple of adjustments. Luca Sbisa's hand had healed and he replaced Jon Merrill on defense. Gallant also sat Tomas Tatar and Tomas Nosek, putting Oscar Lindberg in the lineup instead. Lindberg had a great first month of the season but was quiet thereafter. Gallant was hoping he could help get things turned around.

Merrill had been struggling in the series, and Sbisa was a more experienced player. So it was a slightly different look to the Knights as they skated on the T-Mobile ice for Game 5. They needed to re-establish their team speed through the neutral zone and do a better job of forechecking in the San Jose end if they were going to win this series.

This memo the players got. After attacking from the start, the Knights were rewarded as Neal scored with three seconds left in the opening period. Shea Theodore had fired from the point after being set up by Perron, who was back playing with Neal and Haula. The rebound came to Neal at the right post and he buried it past Jones for the 1-0 lead.

The Sharks had also been warned to stay out of the box by their coach, but they didn't get the memo — at least not in the second period. Alex Tuch scored on the power play while Hertl sat for interference to make it 2-0 Vegas. Then Haula struck to increase the lead to 3-0 just about nine minutes in. And after Tuch made it 4-0 at the 8:36 mark of the third period with his second of the game and fourth of the postseason, DeBoer decided to pull Jones and get him rested up for Game 6, which could be an elimination game for his team.

The Sharks got as close as 4-3 after Mikkel Boedker scored with 4:16 to play. Maybe the elimination game was going to be Vegas' burden as the Sharks pushed hard to get the equalizer and perhaps force overtime for the third straight game. Instead, Marchessault found the empty net with 1:21 to play and the Knights prevailed 5-3 in Game 5. They had a 3-2 series lead with a chance to wrap it up back in San Jose on May 6.

Gallant was pleased with the way his team responded after suffering its first shutout of the postseason. He also liked the way the Knights kept their poise after the Sharks had come back to pull within a goal. Still, he wasn't 100 percent satisfied.

"The other night we played okay, but it wasn't good enough to win. You're not gonna win many games in the playoffs if you don't play your best hockey," Gallant said. "Tonight we came out for 50 minutes and played our best hockey and really set the tone. We got into some penalty trouble at the end and gave them a chance to get back in the game."

But Gallant pushed all the right buttons and his players were feeling good about things after the win.

"I think we turned the page pretty well," said Perron, who had two assists. "We haven't gone on a losing streak too much.

Having said that, it's not going to be easy (in the) next game. We're going to have to provide our best effort.

"It was good to win in front of our crowd, knowing that for sure we're going to get another crack at it no matter what. At the same time, we've got to try and find a way to close it next game."

Neal said: "I think we've been good at regrouping and letting things go, and refocusing and having a big game. You work all year to have home-ice advantage, and we play well at home. Use that for us and I thought coming home we were focusing this morning and it carried over into tonight. I thought we had a great start to our game and a great second period, too.

"We just can't lay off the gas. We've got to continue to play forward, play an honest game and we'll learn from it."

Tuch said: "We were physical, we played hard. It was a good game for everyone."

As Game 6 approached in San Jose on May 6, the Knights were a confident bunch. Yes, they had gotten drilled the last time they played at the SAP Center. But they had also won there, and they had closed out the Kings in the first round in the enemy's barn. But if they were going to win and advance they would have to play faster, play smarter and keep the pressure on the Sharks, who no doubt would be playing with desperation.

They would also have to win without Will Carrier, who had taken a hard hit in the first period of Game 5 and was out with an upper-body injury. The Knights, like most teams, were reluctant to reveal the nature of any injury during the regular season. They were afraid if the other team knew they would target that injury.

As General Manager George McPhee said back in March after Reilly Smith got hurt in Columbus, "I have to protect my players." So if the team wasn't forthright during the regular season in revealing the nature of the injury one of its players had sustained, imagine the subterfuge posture it would take during the playoffs. Even Gallant, who normally would try to help the media understand what was going on in the training room, was tight-lipped.

So with Carrier out, Gallant turned to Ryan Reaves, who had yet to appear in the postseason but who could provide the same level of toughness as Carrier, the team's leader in hits among forwards. Reaves skated on the fourth line with Bellemare and Lindberg, who was taking Tomas Nosek's spot for the second straight game.

The Sharks responded as their fans had hoped, taking the play to the Knights and Fleury, who was making his 10th straight playoff start. The Knights found themselves shorthanded twice in the game's first 9:23 as Haula, then McNabb, were sent off. McNabb was penalized for delay of game after he inadvertently put the puck over the glass although the puck had deflected off the glass before leaving the playing surface. The Sharks had hit the post twice and had three other high-danger scoring chances, but Fleury was up to the task and turned aside all 11 shots he faced during the opening 20 minutes.

If the Knights were going to win, it would be up to their top line to show the way. And that's exactly what happened as Marchessault was set up by Smith after Karlsson forced a turnover by Marc-Edouard Vlasic, San Jose's usually reliable defenseman. Karlsson got the puck to Smith who saw

Marchesssault all alone at the right doorstep. Marchessault took care of the rest, and the Knights had drawn first blood.

But the big goal was yet to come. And it would be Nate Schmidt who would deliver. With just under five minutes to play in the second period, there was a face-off in the San Jose zone and Haula, normally the center, was chased out of the circle and replaced by Perron. He won it back to Schmidt at the point, and Schmidt unleashed a wrist shot that went off Jones, off the post, hit the underside of the crossbar and crossed the goal line before careening back into play.

All goals are reviewed by the NHL's hockey operations department in Toronto. And after looking at it a couple of times, it was determined that Schmidt had scored.

"I had no idea it went in," Schmidt said of his goal. "It's something that happens in playoff hockey. There's more traffic going to the front of the net and it's tough for the goalie to see. So you throw it at the net and sometimes you catch a lucky bounce."

Gallant said of the play: "It was a huge goal. We didn't know on the bench whether or not it was in. But then (video coach) Tommy Cruz signaled us. Two seconds later Toronto called and they got it right. There's obviously a big difference between 1-0 and 2-0."

Faced with a two-goal deficit and just over a period remaining, the Sharks were in the worst-possible position. They were having to chase an elimination game, and all the pressure was on them. Never mind they were at home and DeBoer had the last change. None of that mattered at this point. And given their bad luck so far and the way Fleury was playing, San Jose's task of extending its season was getting tougher and tougher.

But the Knights didn't lay back and play Katie-bar-the-door. They continued to attack and controlled play in the third period. They had seen San Jose mount comebacks in this series, and they were determined not to let it happen again. Then with under two minutes to play and Jones having been pulled for a sixth attacker, Carpenter, the former Shark, helped seal the win with a strong forecheck that led to the puck winding up on his stick. He passed it to Cody Eakin who tapped it into the empty net.

Moments later, it was over. The Knights had won 3-0, took the series four games to two, and once again, they had clinched on the other team's ice.

"We learned our lesson after the last game by not sitting back," Schmidt said. "It's almost like we were playing boring hockey, chipping it in. We were playing a way that just wore them down, I think."

Gallant loved the response by his team.

"I thought the last 10 minutes of the second, and the third period, was outstanding," he said. "It was probably our best hockey of the whole playoffs, to be honest with you. We weren't scoring a whole lot of goals at that time, but we were just playing real good, solid hockey and not giving much at all."

In the loser's locker room, all the Sharks could do is tap their sticks toward the Knights.

"I thought we were the hardest working team in the league coming into the series," DeBoer said. "And that team, I thought, works every single night for (Gallant) and his staff."

Back in Las Vegas, the eighth "X" had been placed on the scoreboard hanging in the team's offices at City National Arena. They were headed to the Western Conference Finals.

More important, the Golden Knights were halfway to the Stanley Cup.

18. Conference Champions

Stanley Cup fever had gripped Southern Nevada. With the Golden Knights having reached the Western Conference Finals, fans were jumping on the bandwagon. And even those who didn't know a red line from a blue line were now following the team's pursuit of the Cup.

At City National Arena, the team's practice facility, fans were lining up hours before practice to insure themselves of a spot. Another line formed daily outside the team's store to snatch up souvenirs, shirts and hats. The Knights were hot. Media representatives from all over the world were coming to Las Vegas to follow the story.

For coach Gerard Gallant and his players the added attention didn't faze them. Their "one day at a time" approach was monotonous but effective, and they weren't about to stray from the path at this point. Nobody in the dressing room was talking Stanley Cup. Instead, it was all about maintaining what they had been doing and finding a way to win Game 1.

The Winnipeg Jets had made a strong second-half run in the regular season to become one of the NHL's top teams. They were talented, young, well-coached and built to be contenders for the Stanley Cup. The team had relocated from Atlanta in 2011 after a second failed attempt to make hockey work in

Georgia. It was also Winnipeg's second go-round in the NHL, after the original Jets moved to Phoenix in 1996 and became the Coyotes.

The Jets had never been this far in the playoffs. But they looked good while dispatching Minnesota in five games during the first round, then battled Nashville and prevailed in a hard-fought, seven-game series to get to the conference finals.

They had their own hot goalie in Connor Hellebuyck, who was a finalist for the Vezina Trophy, which is awarded to the NHL's top goaltender. They also had one of the game's rising superstars in forward Patrik Laine, who was taken second overall in the 2016 draft and who possessed a hard, quick shot. Laine was a danger to score anywhere on the ice.

Winnipeg plays in the smallest building in the entire NHL, the MTS Bell Place which seats only 15,294. But every game sells out. The fan base was passionate and smart. They knew hockey and it can be an intimidating place for opposing teams to play.

It also is the home of the "Whiteout." The Jets encourage their fans to wear white to all home playoff games, a tradition that started back in 1987. Over the decades, teams in other sports have copied the Jets, providing T-shirts, rally towels and encouraging their fans to show up to games in a designated color.

It was also a far cry from the early 1960s, when the NHL was a six-team league and men came to games dressed in suits and ties, and women wore dresses, as if they were attending the opera or the theater instead of a sporting event.

The last time the Knights were in Winnipeg it was the beginning of February. The wind chill was 24 below zero, and there was snow everywhere. It was a different kind of whiteout. Now, as they prepared to drop the puck for Game 1 on May 12, the temperature had warmed up considerably. It was 73 degrees and people had traded in their parkas and boots for shorts and flip-flops.

"We know what they bring. We know that they're good, that they maybe surprised a few teams, but not really," said Paul Stastny, who the Jets had acquired at the trade deadline from St. Louis back in February. He had fit in seamlessly with Winnipeg. "They had 109 points. In a sense they play like us. They have a lot of depth, they can roll four lines, and they have good, puck-moving D. So we're going to have our hands full for sure."

The Knights were expecting a battle.

"They're a fast team, and they have a lot of offense for sure," said forward Jonathan Marchessault. "They have unbelievable players on that roster, and it will definitely be a tough task for sure."

The Knights had been most successful when they scored first. But as the series got underway, it was Winnipeg which took the lead when defenseman Dustin Byfuglien ripped a slap shot past Marc-Andre Fleury off an odd-man rush, just 1:05 into Game 1. It quickly became a 2-0 game as Laine scored on a power play while Alex Tuch sat for hooking. Less than a minute later, Joel Armia, a member of Winnipeg's fourth line, made it 3-0 as he was left unattended in front of Fleury, who had no chance to make the save.

The Knights got one back 35 seconds later as Brayden McNabb scored his team's first goal of the series. Marchessault had set him up at the right face-off circle, and Hellebuyck never saw McNabb with the puck until it was too late. It was 3-1, and two and a half periods still remained. The Knights had come back from two-goal deficits before. Nobody was panicking in the cramped visitors' locker room.

In the home team room, the Jets, obviously encouraged by their fast start, weren't about to take their foot off the gas pedal. They knew how teams can come back. They themselves had done it in the previous series against Nashville, rallying from 3-0 down to win 7-4 in Game 3. So the next goal would be big.

Midway through the second period, Mark Scheifele delivered. The Jets' talented veteran center scored on a power play to make it 4-1. Now the Knights were chasing the game, and a late-period goal from William Karlsson wouldn't be enough. Winnipeg clamped down defensively and with the approval of the 15,321 in the barn went on to win 4-2 and take a 1-0 lead in the best-of-seven series.

The Jets, who had a day's rest, still had momentum from beating the Predators, while the Knights, who had six days between games after defeating the Sharks, may have been a tad out of sync.

"We didn't have much of a rest, we're still in game mode," Byfuglien said. "It was just a matter of coming out, playing our game, keeping it simple. We got in moving our feet right away, ice opened up, so we got to move the puck easily, just do simple things."

Marchessault, who assisted on both Vegas goals, said his team needed to play better and that Game 2 would tell what the Knights were really made of.

"Not the start we wanted, and they just played two days ago, but they were game ready and we weren't," he said. "We're going to see what kind of team we are. Monday is definitely a must-win game."

Yes and no. Yes, the Knights would be in great shape if they could win Game 2. They would get the much-desired split on the road. They would get home-ice advantage, and they might swing the momentum in their direction.

No, it wouldn't be the end of the world if they lost. They would be down 0-2 in the series, but if they could hold serve in their rink, they would just have to find a way to eventually win a game in Winnipeg in order to advance to the Stanley Cup Final.

The team was upbeat the morning of May 14 as they skated prior to Game 2 later that evening. Nobody was talking about pressure. They had won here back on February 1. But there was going to be a different look to Gallant's lineup. David Perron was not feeling well, and he would not play. Tomas Tatar, who had been yanked for Perron back in the opening round and hadn't played since, was taking Perron's spot. Will Carrier was still out with his upper-body injury, and Ryan Reaves remained in the lineup.

Tatar was brought in to boost the team's offense, and thus far he had failed to deliver. Now he was being counted on to score, and just over 13 minutes into the first period he got the Knights on the board as he put home a rebound of his own shot after he had successfully kept the play alive in the Winnipeg zone.

"I wouldn't say frustrated," Tatar said of watching games from the press box. "It's more that you want to help the team any way you can, and it's just beating you up when you're in the stands and some stuff doesn't go our way.

"We're here all for one goal. We want to win the Cup and we're all doing everything we can to do it. If that's the choice (Gallant makes), you have to respect it and be a good teammate and help motivate the guys as much as you can. It's not easy, but I've been working at practice to try to be ready for an opportunity like this."

The goal gave the Knights an emotional lift. The entire bench perked up, and when Marchessault scored four minutes later to make it 2-0. you could feel the air come out of the Bell MTS Place, not to mention the 22,000 or so who were clad in white and had gathered in a plaza outside the building to watch and be part of the festivities.

It was still 2-0 going into the third period. The Jets had been a bit unlucky, having hit the post and crossbar, and Fleury had bounced back with a strong effort over the first 40 minutes. But Winnipeg got within a goal as Kyle Connor scored just over seven minutes in on a power play while Luca Sbisa sat for tripping. The Jets were very much back in it, and so was their crowd.

But the Knights answered Connor's goal 88 seconds later as Marchessault backed up his words with a beautiful backhand goal to make it 3-1. Reilly Smith drew the Winnipeg defense to him, slipped the puck across to Marchessault on the right side, and Marchessault lifted it over Hellebuyck for his sixth of the playoffs. The Knights picked up their forecheck, the defense kept a clean line of sight in front of Fleury and they stayed out of the penalty box the rest of the way.

And as the final buzzer sounded, it was mission accomplished. A 3-1 win. The series was now tied at 1-1. Home-ice advantage and momentum had shifted to Vegas.

"Every time we (need) a big game out of our group, we show up, and tonight we definitely showed up," Marchessault said. "I think we showed the hockey world that we earned the right to be here, and we're able to play against a great team."

With the series now even and the Knights headed back to T-Mobile Arena for Games 3 and 4 there was renewed optimism among the Vegas fans. Their team was three wins away from playing for the Stanley Cup, and any opportunity to be part of it was not going to be squandered.

Practices became even more crowded in the stands, and the team decided it was going to have to limit capacity because the crowds were creating an unsafe environment. The fire marshal may have also had something to say about it. Wristbands were issued, and once the last wristband was distributed, that was it. The doors to the rink would be closed.

Meanwhile, Jonny Greco, the team's director of entertainment, and his staff were cooking up something special for Game 3. They had already successfully used images on the ice to create special effects, and this time the plan was to "destroy" a jet airplane with a catapult launched from the castle behind the Vegas goal. The opposing team's villain would also magically "disappear" as he was hooked up to a cable and "launched" to the rafters.

The fans loved it. So did NBC, which was televising the series and decided this was too cool not to show its audience. The pregame show, along with Carnell Johnson's rendition of the national anthems (remember, there were now two for him to sing), would be televised.

Country superstar Carrie Underwood, whose husband Mike Fisher played for the Predators, offered her services to the Knights to sing the anthem. A year ago, a bit of a firestorm was created in Music City when the team's regular anthem singer was replaced by a number of country music stars. Some Nashville fans thought it was bad luck to replace the regular singer, and the Predators wound up losing in the Stanley Cup Final to Pittsburgh.

The Knights weren't quite at the Cup Final yet. But they also weren't about to jerk around with their karma. They politely declined Underwood's offer to come to Las Vegas. They had their singer. And when Johnson stepped onto the ice before Game 3 to sing both O Canada and The Star-Spangled Banner, he was given a huge ovation. He was obviously moved as he pounded his chest with his fist and acknowledge the love.

In Winnipeg, when the words "True North" are sung during O Canada, the fans yell out the lyrics, much the way Golden Knights fans yell "Night" during the portion "Gave proof through the night." Johnson paused when he came to the words to allow the Winnipeg fans to chant "True North", and he did the same for "Night" as he had been doing for months.

Game 3 was just 35 seconds old when Marchessault scored on a backhand shot as he was ending his shift. McNabb did a good job of getting to a loose puck in the neutral zone and quickly passed to Marchessault, who eluded a poke check from Hellebuyck and sent the 18,477 spectators into a frenzy, along with the several thousand others who had gathered in Toshiba Plaza to watch the game on a big screen.

To the Jets' credit, they didn't panic. Scheifele scored 5:28 into the second period to tie it 1-1, and Game 3 was very much up for grabs. But James Neal answered Scheifele's goal 12 seconds later, and that may have changed the entire series. For Winnipeg to give up a goal so quickly after it had scored to tie the game was demoralizing. Tuch scored less than five minutes later to make it 3-2. The goal was Tuch's fifth of the playoffs, and he had proved he could deliver when the pressure was on.

More important, Tuch, Neal and Erik Haula were coming through at the right time after being relatively quiet earlier in the series. Haula had made a heads-up play on Neal's goal, knocking down Hellebuyck's attempt to clear the puck from behind his own goal, then feeding Neal for the go-ahead score.

"It was good to get a couple, for sure," Tuch said. "We have a part to do as well, and we haven't gotten enough shots as a line, haven't gotten to the net enough. That's a big emphasis here for us. It's good to get on the board and good to get a win as well. Good to get the confidence going for our line."

The Jets got a second goal from Scheifele to cut it to 3-2 just 18 seconds into the third period. But as was the case in Game 2 when Winnipeg had pulled within a goal, the Knights tightened up defensively, and Fleury would make 14 saves in the final 20 minutes. That was capped off by Marchessault's empty-net goal with three seconds remaining as the Knights won 4-2 in Game 3.

Fleury made 15 saves during a third period that was dominated by the Jets.

"You get Flower as your goaltender, you're going to have chances to win games," Neal said.

Game 4 was two nights later, and with the Knights holding a 2-1 series lead, the plan was the same as Game 3: Get an early lead, feed off the energy of the crowd, let Fleury be Fleury, and don't give the Jets room to do what they do best, which is counterattack and get the puck to their big guns.

Scheifele had been a royal pain so far for Gallant. He would have defenseman Nate Schmidt on the ice whenever Scheifele was out there, but Scheifele had still managed to score in two of the first three games. Gallant still stuck with the plan, and having the last change when it came to personnel, he could put

Schmidt out there whenever Paul Maurice opted to play his star center.

The other concern for Gallant was the number of penalties. His team needed to stay out of the box. The Knights were averaging nearly four trips to the sin bin in the series, and Winnipeg already had three power-play goals.

Game 4 started the way Gallant hoped it would. Karlsson scored 2:25 into the game, thanks to an early power play as Tyler Myers had been called for interference, and the Knights had a 1-0 lead. But the Jets responded with a power-play goal of their own in the second period as Laine scored to tie it 1-1, while Tomas Nosek was sitting for tripping. The penalty was especially painful given it had occurred in the offensive zone. Normally, the offender might find himself sitting for a shift or two to think about how he hurt the team. Instead, Gallant sent Nosek right back out there, and 43 seconds after Laine tied it, Nosek scored to give his team a 2-1 lead. Linemate Pierre-Edouard Bellemare's wrist shot had been stopped by Hellebuyck, but Bellemare alertly followed up his shot and he beat the defense to the rebound. Meanwhile, Nosek parked himself in front of the net. Bellemare saw him unattended, got him the puck and Nosek atoned for his earlier miscue.

"Honestly, I felt relief," Nosek said. "My emotions were built up. I was happy."

The Jets were down but certainly not out. They tied it 5:34 into the third period as Tyler Myers beat Fleury to make it 2-2. Winnipeg now had momentum, and the Jets looked to get the lead. Fleury stayed strong in the Vegas net, and with less than seven minutes to play Smith became the hero as he took advantage of some bad luck on Byfuglien's part. The Jets' defenseman had gotten the puck at the right point and was looking to unleash a slap shot toward Fleury. But he had fanned on the shot and Smith, who was looking to close in, chipped the puck past Byfuglien, easily skated around him and was on a breakaway. He crossed the left face-off circle and unleashed a rising wrist shot that sailed over Hellebuyck's right shoulder and into the net.

It was a fortuitous play to be sure. But it counted just the same, and now staked to a 3-2 lead with 6:58 remaining the Knights turned things over to their goaltender. The Jets were going to play desperate hockey and they attacked every shift. The Knights would try to counterattack and get that coveted insurance goal.

But neither team could score the rest of the way, and as the final buzzer sounded and their fans celebrated, the Knights headed back to their locker room with the knowledge they were one game away from playing for the Stanley Cup. They had taken Winnipeg's best shot. They had been lucky to be sure. But as Branch Rickey, the baseball executive, once said: "Luck is the residue of design."

Fleury had robbed Bryan Little in the second period and had stopped 36 of the 38 shots the Jets threw at him. He was the difference.

"Fleury had to be real good in the third period and he made some unbelievable saves," Gallant said. "We looked a little tired at times but we buckled down and didn't give them any chances. It's all about buckling down, battling hard and having the confidence in yourself to do the job."

The Knights now had control of the best-of-seven series. Game 5 would be Sunday afternoon, May 20, in Winnipeg. As was the case in round one against Los Angeles and round two versus San Jose, the players all said the right things about closing out Winnipeg. Cliches like "The last one is the hardest to win" and, "We can't take our foot off the gas" came from virtually every player's lips. Even Schmidt, who is the most loquacious talker on the team, wasn't straying from the company line.

"Honestly, what's been awesome about our group is we've had much fun in the moment," Schmidt said. "I don't want to fast-forward anything. I don't want to look ahead. I want to be right here, where we are right now, and enjoy this for about five minutes, and then get ourselves ready to go into Winnipeg."

For the Jets and their rabid fans, reality had set in. It was either win three straight or go home for the summer. The franchise had never been this far, and nobody wanted the ride to come to an end. But they also knew there was a stern challenge confronting them, and like the Knights said the right things in their locker room after Game 4, the Jets' players were echoing predictable comments prior to Game 5, cliches like "We're not conceding anything" and, "It's not over until they win four."

The Knights had David Perron back for Game 4, and he was in the lineup for Game 5 as Tomas Tatar, one of the heroes of Game 2, sat in the press box. Will Carrier was still not ready to return, and Ryan Reaves, who had played well in his place, remained on the fourth line with Bellemare and Nosek. Reaves, who is from Winnipeg and who grew up rooting for the Jets as a kid, was now the enemy, and he accepted that. Same for Cody Eakin, who also was raised in the 'Peg.

It was 1-1 after the first period as Tuch had scored for Vegas 5:11 in, only to have Josh Morrissey answer for the Jets. You could feel the tension in the Bell MTS Place as each minute ticked away. The Knights stayed patient, waiting for that big opportunity, while the Jets kept pushing, trying to get the lead and perhaps control of things. And as the game passed its midway point the chance the Knights were seeking had arrived, and it fell to the most unlikely of heroes.

The fourth line had performed consistently well throughout the season and into the playoffs, even though there were constant changes to it. Gallant had sent Bellemare, Nosek and Reaves over the boards with just under eight minutes to play in the second period, with the idea of maintaining the continuity and momentum. Don't take a penalty. Forecheck smartly and get off the ice. Nosek was pressuring the defense along the boards, won possession and got the puck to Sbisa at the left point. Reaves, meanwhile, skated toward the front of the Winnipeg goal, hoping to screen Hellebuyck and be ready in case Sbisa decided to shoot, and there might be a deflection opportunity or a rebound if Hellebuyck made the first save.

Sbisa doesn't have the velocity on his shot of a Colin Miller or even Brad Hunt. But he's a veteran player who knows how to put the puck on net. And as soon as Nosek got him the puck, he quickly settled it on to the blade of his stick and sent it goalward. Reaves, who was now in position, got his stick on Sbisa's shot and the puck suddenly went a different direction than Hellebuyck anticipated. Before he could react, it was past him and the red light was on.

Reaves skated to the glass at the half-boards and punched it in celebration as his teammates mobbed him. He had spent countless hours practicing tip-ins every day, and he had remained ready in the event Gallant needed him. He had stepped into the lineup for Game 6 against San Jose. Now here in Game 5 his goal had given the Knights a 2-1 lead.

"The whole mentality of this team is 'next man up,' " Reaves said. "We've got a deep team. We've got a lot of good players."

Gallant, who continued to push the right buttons throughout the postseason, said he never thought of not playing Reaves after Carrier was hurt against the Sharks.

"He makes people play quicker," Gallant said of how the 31-year-old Reaves can change the tempo of a game with his size and speed. "He worked hard and always stayed prepared. When we put him in against San Jose he played well for us and he gave me no reason to take him out (against Winnipeg)."

Not only was it Reaves' first goal as a member of the Golden Knights, after he had been traded from Pittsburgh in late February, it came in his hometown with family and friends among the 15,321 inside the arena.

"Hearing the boos after I scored was probably my favorite moment of this series," he said. "It's been a little weird. I have a couple of cousins that came in Jets jerseys; a best friend came in a white T-shirt, so they're going to hear about that after."

The Knights had a 2-1 lead. But Game 5 and the series was far from over. And between periods, Gallant reminded his players to be smart, be aggressive, stay out of the penalty box and keep playing the same game that put them in the lead. But Marchessault didn't get the memo about staying out of the box. He got called for a slashing penalty 45 seconds into the third period, and here was the opening the Jets were seeking. Their power play had shown it could be successful in the conference finals, and with Scheifele, Laine, Byfuglien and Blake Wheeler on the ice, the odds were this game and series could find itself shifting with one shot.

But the Knights' penalty killers were up to the task. They had killed three previous power plays, and now they were blocking shots, getting into passing lanes and Fleury was once again being the last line of defense, though coaches will tell you that goalies are a team's first line of defense when it comes to successfully killing off penalties.

It remained 2-1, because instead of laying back and absorbing Winnipeg's attack the way a boxer would lay on the ropes, the Knights used their speed and continued to forecheck strong in the Jets' end. Their defense supported the forecheck and dominated play in the neutral zone. And as the minutes quickly ticked away, it was Vegas, not Winnipeg, which had control of the action. Hellebuyck was pulled for a sixth attacker, but the Jets were unable to tie it.

The scoreboard read 0:00. It also read Knights 2, Jets 1. The expansion team had won the Western Conference, four games to one. And as NHL deputy commissioner Bill Daly came on to the ice to present the Clarence S. Campbell Bowl, which annually goes to the conference champion, two questions loomed.

One, who would accept the trophy? The Knights did not have a captain. For all intents and purposes, Fleury was the team's de facto captain even though he didn't wear a "C" on his sweater. But the team had talked about it the morning of the game, just in case they won they would have a plan. The decision was for Deryk Engelland, their 36-year-old defenseman and Las Vegas resident, to do the honors.

And as Engelland skated over to the corner to accept the Campbell Bowl, Daly said to him, "I'll bet you didn't expect to be doing this."

The other question was, would Engelland touch the trophy? One of the game's superstitions is you only touch the Stanley Cup. Secondary trophies are considered just that, much like in basketball, where college teams sometimes refrain from cutting down the nets after winning an NCAA regional tournament.

But Engelland gladly picked up the Campbell, displayed it for the photographers just like tennis players and golfers show off their trophies for having won a major tournament, and was quickly joined by his teammates.

However, they didn't linger on the ice with their bounty. They didn't want to be disrespectful to the Jets or their fans. They quickly exited the rink and celebrated in their cramped locker room as players, coaches and staff gathered around the Campbell Bowl for a group photo.

General Manager George McPhee and assistant GM Kelly McCrimmon shook hands and hugged the players and coaches in the hallway while a media hoard made its way into the room to get reaction and interviews.

It was truly a joyous moment for the franchise. But there was one person missing from the celebration. Team majority owner Bill Foley was back in Las Vegas, nursing a cold. He watched history being made from his living room.

Back in Winnipeg, the players credited the Jets for being a formidable opponent. But the enormity of the moment and what they had just accomplished had still not hit most of them.

"It's insane," said Engelland. "Your goal is always to make the playoffs. But if I were to guess I would be sitting here doing this right now, you would be a little skeptical at the time. But once we got rolling and got the season going, we saw that we have a team that can do some damage, and a phenomenal goalie that's going to stop everything. It's been an amazing ride. We just want to keep it going now."

They all credited Fleury for helping them get to this point.

"He has been our best player all year," Eakin said. "You go up and down the lineup and guys have stepped up at different times, but he consistently has been our rock, the guy that has held us in games and made those key stops."

Fleury, in turn, complimented his teammates.

"I think you're only as good as your team," Fleury said. "The guys in front of me have been great and they've been helping me a lot. It's been a lot of fun."

The Jets, frustrated by the fact they could not build on their early 1-0 series lead — and having lost four in a row and their chance at playing for the big prize — could only tip their hats to their opponent.

"It was their time," Wheeler said. "They were the better team."

The Knights were now 12-3 through three rounds of the playoffs.

Next, they were going to play for the Stanley Cup.

19. Playing For The Cup

The Golden Knights' charter airplane touched down in Las Vegas' McCarran International Airport Sunday night. But there was no massive throng of fans to welcome the Western Conference champions home.

Because the team disembarks at the charter terminal, which is essentially off-limits to the general public, fans were not able to gather and cheer their heroes upon their triumphant return from Winnipeg. Any interaction with the players would have to wait awhile as coach Gerard Gallant gave the team a couple of well-deserved days off.

"It's been an awesome ride so far," Gallant said. "We won three series, and we're going to the Stanley Cup Final. But, again, this isn't what we want. We want to win. Every team has got a chance to win now in the NHL. The teams are so close. We're far from satisfied. We've got a big series to get ready for.

"Like I said, it's great to win and it's great to be the Western Conference champions, but that's not what we're here for."

The Knights didn't know yet who their opponent would be. The Eastern Conference Finals were a back-and-forth battle between the Tampa Bay Lightning and the Washington Capitals. And as Game 6 approached on Monday, May 21, in Washington, the Lightning held a 3-2 lead in the series. If Tampa prevailed, it would have home-ice in the Stanley Cup

Final. If the Capitals came back and won, the Knights would have home ice.

Both teams had superstars from Russia. The Lightning had Nikita Kucherov; the Capitals had Alex Ovechkin. Both teams also had strong supporting casts, and the Lightning, despite holding the lead in the best-of-seven series, was far from a lock to get to the Final.

The Capitals wound up winning Game 6, 3-0 as Braden Holtby played a sensational game in the Washington net. Holtby had sat on the bench for the first two games of the playoffs against Columbus. But coach Barry Trotz put him in after the Blue Jackets had taken a 2-0 lead in the opening-round series. Now, with the deciding Game 7 at Amalie Arena in Tampa, Holtby would be the key.

He turned aside all 29 shots he faced in Game 7, and Ovechkin's goal 1:02 into the contest stood up as the Capitals blanked the Lightning for the second straight game, this time 4-0. They would play for the Stanley Cup for only the second time in the club's 44-year history. This was a franchise that was the epitome of futility among expansion teams, having won a record-low eight games in 1974-75 while playing in suburban Landover, Maryland. They were the polar opposite of the Golden Knights.

The previous Capitals team that made it to the Cup Final was in 1998. George McPhee was in his first year as general manager of the franchise then, and he would know the feeling of coming close but not quite getting there. The Caps had been swept by the Detroit Red Wings in four games and they had not been back since.

McPhee rebuilt the franchise twice, and it was the handiwork of his second go-round that had Washington in the

2018 Cup Final. Twelve players on the roster were the result of either the draft, trades or free agent signings during his tenure, and McPhee was proud of what he had accomplished.

The Knights' GM is not one to bring the spotlight upon himself. He limits his time in front of the media and prefers to do his job privately. But on the eve of Game 1 he addressed his time in Washington and what he had done in Vegas.

"I'm certainly proud of the Washington team and the players," McPhee said. "Really happy for them — and really proud of this team we have in Vegas.

"It's funny how life goes. Two years ago I was walking around Ann Arbor kicking stones and couldn't get a job."

Brian McClellan, who was McPhee's assistant in Washington and is the Capitals' current general manager, said of the juxtaposition of going up against his longtime friend and former boss in the Final: "It's kind of a weird experience. It's a little awkward, but it's going to be a fun experience — I hope."

Gallant still didn't have Will Carrier for his fourth line. And he still didn't have Malcolm Subban as his backup goaltender. Subban had sprained his ankle during practice in the Western Conference Finals, and Maxime Lagace was once again called upon to serve as Fleury's understudy. Fleury had played every minute of every one of the team's 15 playoff games to date. He said he felt fine and there was no fatigue factor to deal with. Gallant gave him an extra day off between the conference finals and the Cup Final, and Fleury was ready to go when it began on Monday, May 28.

Memorial Day weekend was coming to a close, and that is always a busy time in Las Vegas as visitors, especially from California, flock to the city for fun.

But now there was an added element. The city was hosting the Stanley Cup Final, and as a result, NBC was in town. And if NBC was in town, it meant Mike "Doc" Emrick was behind the microphone, calling the play-by-play.

Emrick was one of sports' pre-eminent announcers. He had a room full of Emmy Awards and was in several halls of fame, including the Hockey Hall of Fame. At the age of 71, Emrick was still very much on top of his game. But he had also never called a Golden Knights game. So he had a kid's excitement and curiosity as he visited City National Arena for the team's morning skate prior to Game 1.

He saw the stands packed with fans chanting "Go Knights Go!". He saw fans with their dogs, including Bark-Andre Furry, the Jack Russell terrier who had gained a high level of celebrity during the season and had come face-to-face with the Knights' goalie during the year.

"Nice dog," Fleury said of Furry, who by now had been outfitted with a pair of mini goalie pads to go with his Golden Knights' No. 29 "sweater".

It was a small sample of what Emrick would encounter a few hours later, and he told the Las Vegas Review-Journal's Ron Kantowski, "I'm just looking forward to listening to the crowd."

Emrick was part of a special team. He was a cancer survivor going back to 1991. His broadcast partners, Ed Olczyk and Pierre McGuire, had also battled cancer, and both of them were back on the job. They would tell the story of the Golden Knights to those who were still unfamiliar.

Hockey — unlike football, basketball and baseball — still didn't have the kind of audience that could reach beyond its own sport's grasp. Yes, the numbers had increased. Ratings were better and attendance was still excellent in the majority of the league's arenas. The Knights had played beyond their capacity at T-Mobile Arena and Commissioner Gary Bettman said it was a story for the ages.

"Nobody saw this coming," Bettman said. "George McPhee and (assistant GM) Kelly McCrimmon did an outstanding job. The bond is real between this city and its first-ever major league professional sports team. The connection is undeniable. This is the magic of sports. Anything can happen."

The same held true for the pregame entertainment. With the Golden Knights, you could never predict what Jonny Greco and his staff were capable of doing. And given this was the Stanley Cup Final, something cool was expected.

The NHL has to approve everything. And when it was suggested the Imagine Dragons, a Las Vegas-based rock band which had earned world-wide acclaim and had an international fan base, was chosen to provide some of the music, it was well received. The Dragons performed their big hit, "Whatever It Takes", and the moving performance by lead singer Dan Reynolds brought down the house.

For the starting lineups, the Knights called upon Michael Buffer, the hall of fame boxing ring announcer, to do the honors. Buffer, best known for his trademark phrase, "Let's Get Ready To Rumble", introduced both teams the way he would a world championship title fight. It was cool and humorous and the fans loved it.

Gallant and his players were looking to create some more magic. And when Collin Miller scored the first goal of the Final just 7:15 into the game, and T-Mobile Arena went berserk, it appeared that was going to be the case.

But the Capitals hadn't reached this point through luck alone. They had skill and talent, and they took a 2-1 lead with less than five minutes to go in the first period as Brett Connolly and Nicklas Backstrom scored. Backstrom was playing with a broken finger on his right hand, and some were curious as to how effective he could be. But he is one of the game's best passers and he's highly intelligent. He can make plays from anywhere on the ice, healthy or injured.

By now the Knights had dealt with coming back numerous times, and William Karlsson delivered with the game-tying goal with 1:41 left in the period. Reilly Smith managed to find him by using his great peripheral vision. Smith then broke the 2-2 tie 3:21 into the second period as he beat Braden Holtby, and Vegas again had the lead back 3-2.

But back came the Caps. John Carlson scored from the point on a shot Fleury admitted he should have stopped to tie the game 3-3. Then tough guy Tom Wilson put Washington back in front as he was left alone in front of the net 1:10 into the third period, and the Caps had a 4-3 lead.

As they had done against Winnipeg, the Knights immediately answered. Ryan Reaves, the hero of the series clincher against the Jets, was in the right place at the right time. Tomas Nosek's shot attempt came back to Reaves. And after a second swipe was unsuccessful, and defenseman Michal Kempny failed to clear the puck, Reaves pounced and beat Holtby to pull Vegas even 4-4. The goal had come 91 seconds after Wilson's.

Now the Knights had renewed energy, and once again the fourth line would deliver at the midway point of the final period. Shea Theodore had kept the play alive in the Washington zone, and Nosek had eluded John Carlson and was all alone at the right post. Theodore saw Nosek and hit him with a perfect pass. Nosek one-timed it past Holtby, who never saw him.

The Knights were now back in front in what had turned into a wild, back-and-forth affair during which the lead changed four times. Fleury made sure there would not be a fifth change as he stopped the Capitals time and again. Nosek sealed Game 1 with an empty-net goal with three seconds remaining, and the Knights had held serve on home ice with a 6-4 victory.

"It's great when you see those guys get rewarded," Gallant said of Reaves and Nosek. "That fourth line went out there and battled hard and got pucks down below the goal line."

"We put fun ahead of everything, and you can tell," Reaves said. "Guys are having fun and they're smiling."

But there was also controversy to deal with in the aftermath. Wilson had leveled Marchessault with a blind-side check that forced the Knights' top scorer out of the game and to the locker room where he underwent concussion protocol. Wilson, a repeat offender when it came to crossing the line, claimed he didn't do anything illegal.

The play came less than six minutes into the third period. Marchessault didn't have the puck and Wilson could have chosen to avoid contact. But he leveled Marchessault and wound up going to the penalty box for interference. Marchessault would return to the game. But afterward, he still wasn't happy with the hit.

"I saw the hit. I remember everything," he said. "It was a late hit. I don't really need to talk more about it. I think the league will take care of it. We know what type of player he is out there. You gotta keep your head up and try to make the play. I didn't make the play. It was a little late, but whatever."

More important, would Wilson get a call from George Parros, who headed up the NHL's Department of Player Safety? Wilson had already been suspended once during the playoffs for a hit on the Penguins' Zach Aston-Reese, which resulted in the Pittsburgh forward suffering a broken jaw. Wilson got four games for that incident. Gallant hoped the league would do something.

"I didn't like it," he said after the game. "It was a late hit."

Reaves, a tough guy in his own right, said: "That's Wilson being Wilson."

Caps coach Barry Trotz made a prediction regarding Wilson.

"I expect him to play in Game 2," he said.

Trotz would be right. The NHL took no further disciplinary action against Wilson and both teams moved on from the matter. But would there be payback and would Reaves be the one to deliver it?

There was one other issue heading into Game 2 on May 30. The ice at T-Mobile Arena, which had been consistently excellent throughout the season as well as during the first three rounds of the playoffs, appeared to present some problems in Game 1. Numerous times during stoppages of play members of the team's ice maintenance staff had to come out and patch up areas of the ice near both blue lines where the blue "Stanley Cup Final" logos had been painted in. Players from both teams complained about the quality of the ice, and after the game, Dan Craig, the NHL's ice guru, was seen conferring with George Salami, who is in charge of the ice in the building.

It had been hot all day, and with the doors to the arena constantly open to allow the entrance of equipment and other items, not to mention nearly 19,000 spectators emitting heat from their bodies, the ice may have deteriorated somewhat. The arena had hosted a concert Saturday featuring pop star Pink. And the ice, which had been redone to accommodate the new logos, was still somewhat fresh and not quite broken in by game-time Monday.

Salami defended his sheet, claiming there was nothing wrong with the ice. Nonetheless, there were going to be some adjustments made for Game 2.

As was the case in Game 1, the Knights jumped out to a 1-0 lead as James Neal took advantage of a miscue by defenseman Dmitry Orlov and scored on Holtby 7:58 into the first period. And as was the case in Game 1, here came Washington to retake the lead. Lars Eller, the Capitals' underrated third line center, beat Fleury from close range with 2:32 remaining and it was 1-1 going into the second period. Ovechkin then cashed in on a power play while Tuch was sitting in the box for cross-checking to give the Caps a 2-1 lead. Just over four minutes later, Brooks Orpik made it 3-1 as he beat Fleury from the point. Orpik hadn't scored a goal in more than two years, and he was the most unlikely of candidates to be a goal-scoring hero. Put it this way, no one was confusing Orpik with Ovechkin when it came to lighting the lamp.

The Knights managed to pull within a goal late in the second as Theodore scored on a power play with T.J. Oshie in the box for interference. And with the entire third period still to play and trailing only 3-2, there was no need to get overly concerned. A one-goal deficit was hardly insurmountable. Besides, the Knights had been great at home all year. Their fans remained very much engaged and the Knights emerged from their locker room for the final 20 minutes with positive vibes and brimming with confidence.

But the Capitals were a confident bunch, too. They knew what this game meant. If they held on and won, they would get a split on the road, get home-ice advantage, and they would be putting themselves in a most advantageous position.

Still, it was Vegas and not Washington which played with desperation. The Knights continued to attack, forecheck hard and pressure Holtby, who was coming up big time after time, especially during a critical 5-on-3 Vegas advantage early in the third period.

Now, with just over two minutes to play and the his team clinging to the one-goal lead, Holtby would be called on at least one more time to bail out the Caps. The Knights had sent the puck into the Washington zone and it had taken a weird bounce off the side of the net. The puck came to Cody Eakin who was on the right side of the goal. Eakins had time to pass or shoot, and as he was deciding what to do, here came Tuch all alone headed toward the left post. Holtby was focusing on Eakin, who still had possession. Suddenly, Eakin put his pass to Tuch right on the tape and Tuch had nothing but an open net to shoot at. He was about to atone for his second-period penalty which Ovechkin scored during the power play.

Tuch elevated the puck slightly, and they were getting ready to hit the goal horn sound effect in the press box. But Holtby kept the horn silent. He dove to his right, extended the paddle of his goaltender's stick and got a piece of Tuch's shot.

It was an incredible save, one that would be etched into Stanley Cup lore. On NBC, Pierre McGuire proclaimed, "In Washington, that will forever be known as 'The Save'".

The Capitals still led 3-2. But there were still two minutes left and the Knights weren't dead yet. They pulled Fleury for a sixth attacker, and James Neal had two glorious chances. Colin Miller had a great chance as well. But none of their shots crossed the goal line. Washington held on for the 3-2 win, and the Caps left Las Vegas with home-ice advantage and a split in the first two games of the best-of-seven Final.

"It was a strange play because these boards have been really true," Holtby said in explaining "The Save" on Tuch. "It was kind of one of those things is we've been trying to get it up on the glass at our rims because usually goalies stay in their net. But Marc-Andre's been coming out a lot to get those because they've been so true, and one bounces weird at that time of the game. (Eakin) makes a great play to pass it over and I was just trying to get something there, trying to seal where I thought someone would shoot that. And luckily it hit me."

Trotz said a higher power was looking out for his goalie.

"To me, it was the hockey gods," he said. "They evened it up from last game. They (the Knights) could've tied it up but they didn't. I thought Braden was really good. I just think they played it the right way. Hockey gods always sort of even that out. I always talk about that. It was a great save, and honestly there was about 1:59 left. You could see the emotion on our bench. Once he made that save, I knew we were going to win the game."

Tuch was philosophical in describing his feelings, saying, "He made a great save."

It was also the understatement of the 21st Century.

While the Capitals were thrilled to be going home tied in the series, they were concerned about one of their stars. Evgeny Kuznetsov, their leading scorer, had injured his left arm after being hit by Brayden McNabb in the first period and did not return. Game 3 was not until Saturday, June 2, so he'd have an extra day to heal up.

The Caps were no less pleased with the hit to Kuznetsov as the Knights were with Wilson's hit on Marchesssault in Game 1. But like Wilson, McNabb faced no supplemental discipline for the Kuznetsov hit. And when the Caps skated in the warmups at Capital One Arena, No. 92 in red was on the ice.

After they dropped the puck to begin Game 3, No. 8 took over. Just 70 seconds into the contest, Ovechkin ripped a shot past Fleury for a 1-0 Washington lead. As had been the case at T-Mobile when Miller scored first in Game 1, Ovechkin's goal amped the home crowd even more.

And, in a bit of poetic justice, Kuznetsov scored past the midway point of the second period to give the Caps a 2-0 lead. It was still 2-0 heading into the third period, but the Capitals were doing a great job of limiting the high-scoring opportunities the Knights had so successfully created all season and during the playoffs. They had the speed to contain the Knights in the neutral zone and their defensemen and forwards were doing a great job of blocking shots. Even Ovechkin got in on the act.

The Knights managed to get back in it as Nosek scored his fourth of the playoffs to cut it to 2-1 at 3:29 of the third. Plenty of time remained and nobody was panicking on the Vegas bench. Gallant continued to roll his lines out, and he hoped one of them would find a way to get one past Holtby.

But it wasn't to be. The Caps were the ones who were opportunistic as Devante Smith-Pelly and Jay Beagle teamed up and Smith-Pelly scored the insurance goal with just over six minutes remaining to give the Caps a 3-1 lead. That would be the final score as Washington took a 2-1 series lead. The Caps also had 26 blocked shots with 14 different players having blocked at least one Vegas shot.

More important, Trotz's adjustments forced the Knights to abandon their slick passing game and revert to a dump-and-chase mode. It wasn't the way they liked to play, but with Washington able to negate Vegas' overall team speed and use an effective forecheck, it changed the tenor of the game.

"I want us to play fast, play a quick game," Gallant said. "I think the biggest problem is we're in the offensive zone and turning pucks over down there. We're throwing pucks at the net and not getting pucks to the net. They're taking the puck from the offensive zone. Their D are joining the rush and they get a four-man attack. That's one of the biggest reasons. It's not turning the puck over in the neutral zone; it's turning it over in the offensive zone. We have to make sure we're strong on the puck, take it to the net more."

Game 4 was Monday, June 4, and Gallant was shuffling the deck again, trying to jump-start his team. Perron was a healthy scratch, and Tomas Tatar was back in. Perron had failed to score in the playoffs, and though Tatar had the one goal in Winnipeg, Gallant felt he might be a better option when it came to generating some offense.

As Game 4 got underway, it quickly became evident that Lady Luck was not with the Knights. Tuch hit the post early on, then Neal had an open net, and he hit the post instead. If either shot went in, the Knights might have been sitting pretty, or at least they might have been playing from in front.

"It probably changes the game," Neal said. "It's probably a different game after that. I had a wide-open net, and I just hit the post."

Instead, the Capitals scored three times over a 9:11 first-period span to lead 3-0. It became 4-0 late in the second period as Carlson scored on a Washington power play. Things were getting out of hand. Would Gallant consider yanking Fleury to rest him for what was now shaping up as an elimination Game 5?

Fleury stayed in the Vegas net and his teammates battled to make it respectable. Neal scored 5:43 into the third period and Reilly Smith added a goal less than seven minutes later to reduce the deficit to 4-2. But Kempny scored 1:13 after Smith to make it 5-2. Connolly closed it out with a power-play goal and a 6-2 Washington victory.

Things got a little chippy late in the game as Oshie broke Miller's nose after getting his stick up in his face, and a big scrum broke out in the Vegas zone as Oshie mixed it up with McNabb and Engelland. It didn't change the outcome, however. The Caps had held serve at home and had a 3-1 series lead. They were one win away from the franchise's first Stanley Cup.

"We obviously got some breaks at the start of the game," Holtby said. "Honestly, I thought (Neal's shot) was in, from my angle, and somehow it didn't go in."

The Knights were facing elimination for the first time, but they would try to stay alive at home. They still hadn't found a way to get more high-grade chances against Holtby. The Caps held a 24-8 edge in blocked shots, and it doesn't help when you can't hit an open net.

Vegas had not lost more than three straight games at any juncture in the franchise's brief history. Now, the Knights were faced with the harsh reality — if they lose a fourth straight, they won't get a chance to play again until October.

The talk was not to try and win three games, but one. And not trying to win one game, but win one period. "Shift by shift" was the mantra from the Knights' locker room as they prepared to hit the ice for Game 5. The Capitals weren't thinking too far ahead either. Yes, they had command of the series. Yes, they knew they were facing a challenge to close it out on the road. But it was going to be up to the home team to adjust and find a way. Trotz? He wasn't about to change a thing.

The Caps were buoyed by the fact that several thousand of their fans had managed to find their way into the building. Apparently, many Golden Knights fans had decided to break their "Knights Vow" and not resell their tickets on the secondary online markets. For those Washington fans who made the trip to Las Vegas, it was a pricey proposition. Between airline tickets, hotels, food and drink, and game tickets, it was probably costing each of them a few thousand dollars. But what's money when you have a chance to witness your team make history?

Gallant didn't have many cards left to play at this point. But he made two moves. One was to sit Ryan Carpenter and get David Perron back on the ice. The other was that Will Carrier was ready to play. So he was in and Ryan Reaves was out. And as Game 5 got under way, the teams played somewhat cautious, trying not to make that fatal mistake.

It was still scoreless after the first period in which the two teams had combined for just 16 shots. That was fine with the Caps. They were playing with house money at this point, and should they fall behind and ultimately lose Game 5, they still had two more opportunities to win the Cup. The Knights did not enjoy such a luxury. They had to win. And when Jakob Vrana scored 6:24 into the second period to give Washington a

1-0 lead, everyone inside T-Mobile waited to see what the response would be.

Nate Schmidt, the former Capitals defenseman, said he and his teammates simply had to play better if they were to have any chance of coming back. And a little over three minutes after Vrana had scored, Schmidt tied it 1-1 as Smith set him up. He wristed a shot from inside the blue line which may have gone off a Caps player and past Holtby. Either way, he got credit for the goal, the game was tied 1-1 and the Knights had new life. At least momentarily.

Eleven seconds later, however, the Capitals were on a power play as McNabb was sent off for tripping. And with Ovechkin setting up in his office — at the left face-off circle half-boards — Backstrom got him the puck. Sure enough, Ovechkin fired it past Fleury to put Washington up 2-1. He was making a strong final push to win the Conn Smythe Trophy, which goes to the outstanding performer in the playoffs.

Once, there was talk that Fleury would be the recipient had the Knights won the Stanley Cup. But that talk had long since ceased.

Now the Stanley Cup was headed to T-Mobile Arena. Phil Pritchard and Mike Bolt, the Hockey Hall of Fame employees and longtime "Keepers of the Cup", were in charge of delivering it to the arena in the event it was to be awarded. But the Knights weren't ready for that eventuality. They tied the game a couple of minutes later when Perron was checked into Holtby and fell into the net as the puck hit him. The Caps challenged the goal, claiming interference. But the goal stood and the game was tied at 2-2. It was Perron's first — and last — goal of the postseason.

With 29 seconds left in the period and the Knights on a 5-on-3 power play, Smith scored to give his team a 3-2 lead. And as they headed to their locker room, the Knights knew it would take more to keep the season going. It meant everyone getting involved at both ends of the ice and giving Fleury every opportunity to keep the puck out of his net.

In the Washington locker room, everything was calm. Trotz's message to his guys? Stay patient, play smart, keep working and wait for a break. The Knights were doing a better job of getting quality shots on Holtby as evidenced by the three goals, though Perron's was a bit of a fluke. Still, the Caps continued to block shots, clog the neutral zone and create good chances of their own.

And that persistence finally paid off as Smith-Pelly tied it at the midway point of the third period. He won a battle with Sbisa in the corner, got the puck to Orpik, then went to the front of the net. Miller tried to bat down Orpik's shot with his stick but he missed. Instead, Smith-Pelly had the puck hit his skate, and as he was falling, managed to get the blade of his stick on the puck and lift it over Fleury's glove.

The Capitals had tied it 3-3. Now the pressure was really on Vegas. Yes, there was still half the third period to play and there was always the possibility of sudden death overtime. But that was playing with fire. No, if the Knights were going to keep their season going, they needed to win Game 5 in regulation.

They looked to their top line of Karlsson, Marchessault and Smith to deliver. But the Capitals were hell-bent on not letting the trio beat them. On the flip side, Trotz was getting great play out of his bottom-six forwards because Gallant wasn't about to let Ovechkin, Kuznetsov, Backstrom and Oshie beat his team.

Andre Burakovsky, a member of the third line, had managed to get the puck after Sbisa had overskated it. He fed Connolly, who was cruising the slot, and Connolly's wrist shot was stopped by Fleury. But the puck was behind him and he couldn't locate it. Meanwhile, Sbisa was now in front of the net but not in a position to make a play on the puck and clear it out of the crease. Lars Eller was in position, however. The center of Washington's third line swooped in, and before anyone could react, deposited it into a now-empty cage to give the Capitals a 4-3 lead. The several thousand Caps' fans inside T-Mobile were celebrating along with tens of thousands back in D.C., where the team had opened the doors to Capital One Arena and had also set up a watch party outside nearby.

For both Smith-Pelly and Eller, it was their seventh goal of the playoffs, and both would be a part of history that was being written in Las Vegas. There was still 7:37 to go, and there was time for one last comeback by the home team.

The Capitals took the body, dove at every shot trying to block the puck. Holtby was staying strong in the Washington net, and with the Knights pushing forward as much as they could, trying to keep their season alive, the Capitals managed to maintain their poise and their narrow one-goal lead.

Fleury had been yanked for an extra attacker. But it didn't help. The final seconds ticked away, and as the horn sounded the Capitals raced to their goaltender and mobbed him as the celebration was underway.

After 44 years, the Washington Capitals were Stanley Cup champions. For the Vegas Golden Knights, their improbable, historic, record-setting run was over. They waited at the blue line and then lined up, led by Bellemare, to shake hands with the victors. For the first time as a franchise, the Knights were on the wrong side of the handshake line.

And as they prepared to depart the ice, where they had been so successful, they raised their sticks to their fans, who had stuck around to give them one final standing ovation. Even the thousands of Capitals fans joined in to salute the home team which had provided the hockey world with so many thrills, mindful that the Knights had helped raise the sagging spirits of an entire city after it had endured a horrific tragedy prior to the start of the team's inaugural season.

Ovechkin, who had been drafted as the No. 1 overall pick by George McPhee in 2004, was voted the recipient of the Conn Smythe Trophy as the MVP of the playoffs.

Bettman walked out to make the presentation, and he was roundly booed. He said smart-alecky to the crowd, "Thank you Las Vegas, you truly are an NHL city." But nobody wanted to hear any wisecracks from the commissioner. He proceeded to award the Stanley Cup to Ovechkin, Washington's captain. And as Ovechkin and his Washington teammates celebrated on the T-Mobile ice, McPhee didn't stick around to watch what he had helped create. In his mind, it wasn't right. He retreated to the bowels of the arena and stayed there.

20. Reflections Of An Amazing Run

The Stanley Cup playoff scoreboard banner which hung inside the Golden Knights' offices at City National Arena had come up three X's short. The season was over. And for everyone, from owner Bill Foley to the secretaries and everyone else in the organization, it had been a long, hard journey.

For the players, the pain of having come up short was still fresh as they came to the rink the next morning to conduct their exit interviews, have any medical issues addressed and collect their belongings. Most teams usually take a day or two after the season ends for their exit day. But for the Knights, it had been a long enough year. No sense in delaying the inevitable.

There was talk of holding a parade or a celebration. But the team wasn't interested in any kind of parade. In fact, it tried to distance itself from such talk even before the Stanley Cup Final. City and county officials had begun preliminary planning earlier for such an eventuality. It was considered to be bad luck to talk about celebrating before you won anything, and the team had no interest in being a party to it.

The team would eventually agree to do a postseason celebration at the Fremont Street Experience in downtown Las Vegas a few days later. But it was more of a "Thank You" to the fans for their support. From the players' and coaches' perspectives, there's nothing to celebrate when you're second-best.

To a man, everyone said it was a heck of a season, an amazing run and they were proud to have been part of it. They talked about coming together in training camp, bonding as a team, dealing with the myriad injuries, particularly when it came to the goaltenders.

"It's been an exceptional run, obviously," Gallant said on June 8. "From back in October to today, it's been unbelievable. For us to be playing until June 7th was an incredible story. We just took it one day at a time and one game at a time, all year long. We had an incredible run. We fell a little bit short of the big prize. But it was an unbelievable season. We got the best out of our team and that was really important for us."

Gallant said nobody had been talking Stanley Cup back in September.

"I didn't even think about it," he said. "I don't remember that question being asked at training camp. If they would have said playoffs, I would have laughed a little bit too, but to say the Stanley Cup? I wouldn't have even responded to that question.

"We had an incredible year. From day one there were no expectations about playoffs, there was no expectation about winning 20 games. It was about coming to play every night. I think I told you, and you are probably sick of me saying it, that it's about the next game. It's not about the game that happened, not the last one. So, we just take it one game at a time.

"We went through 82 games and finished first in our division, which was a great accomplishment for our players," Gallant continued. "They worked hard and they competed hard. You go into the playoffs thinking, you know what? It would be incredible to win a couple of games here and try to win a first round series and it was a great experience for our players. We did an unbelievable job against LA, and to sweep the Kings, who are very good. It was an unbelievable series for our staff and our players. Then you go onto the next series and say, 'San Jose is a real good team' but you didn't fear them. You felt like if you played well you would win, and that's what happened.

"Then you a play a team like Winnipeg, who to me was probably the best team in the NHL this season, and we go into that series, lose Game 1 and then everybody started to count us out.

"We peel out four games and win, to beat Winnipeg. It was an outstanding thing, but it wasn't like I was surprised by the way our team played the second half of the season and the confidence they built over the second half of the season. There wasn't a team that I was afraid of, and that's the way our players were. It didn't matter who we were going to play, if we played well we had a chance to win. That was the feeling with our group."

William Karlsson, who had a career year with 43 goals, said: "We made it almost all the way, and we are going to try to be better next year. That's our goal. I like the roster that we have, and we have the young prospects coming up too and it looks really good. So, the future is bright."

Nate Schmidt, who never kept his feelings inside, said: "It's a great group to be a part of. It makes you happy knowing that when you come back this is going to be the group that's going to be here. This is our guys that you started with, and hopefully have a chance to finish with.

"It's hard because in light of what just happened, but at the same time you look at everything that we have been through and if you look at the city, that's the best part. Even after the game you go and grab a drink, and people are just coming up to us and saying, 'We are proud to have you guys here.' It gives you the chills, and it's the reason why we play. It's not even just being a part of a hockey team, but a part of this community."

Back in training camp, the players looked around the room at each other and branded themselves with the "Golden Misfits" tag James Neal had bestowed upon the group. It was kind of funny, a bit cute and everyone seemed to embrace the concept. After all, they had all come to Las Vegas unwanted by their former teams. Even Gallant, who had been literally kicked to the curb by the Florida Panthers, was a Golden Misfit. Yet they had come together to have one of the most remarkable first seasons in sports history. It was truly one heck of a story and now it was over.

For some players, it was the last time they would step foot in the locker room. Free agency was looming and the Knights had four unrestricted free agents to deal with, including Neal and David Perron. Together, the duo had combined for 31 goals and 110 points, most of the time playing on the same line. Luca Sbisa and Ryan Reaves were also UFAs, and they also faced uncertain futures in Las Vegas.

George McPhee had to figure out how to handle Karlsson, who was a restricted free agent. The general manager could make Karlsson a qualifying offer at 105 percent of what he made in 2017-18. He also had similar situations with Colin Miller, Shea Theodore, Tomas Nosek and Will Carrier.

"Well, you have to be really smart on all of the deals that you do," McPhee told the media on exit day. "It doesn't matter where in the lineup you're looking at, you have to be smart about what you do.

"We have all of these resources now and we're in a cap world. You have to trust your instincts as a management group. You have to trust the reports from your pro scouting staff and you have to trust the data that you're getting from your analytics group. That's something that we didn't have years ago and we have now. It tells you certain things and you have to pay attention. We put it all together and try to make the right decisions.

"Mistakes happen, and you don't want to be a part of them," McPhee continued. "They only get in the way of winning. There are different ways to make a team better. You look at all of the different resources and ways to do that, and figure out how we make this team better for next year."

One of those ways is through the draft. The NHL Entry Draft was also rapidly approaching, and unlike a year ago, when the Knights had three picks in the first 15 selections, this year they would go to Dallas on June 22 without a first-round pick. Vegas had traded that pick to Detroit for Tomas Tatar, and as it turned out the Red Wings would pick 30th with the selection. From McPhee's perspective it wasn't that big a deal if the Knights didn't have a first-round pick. There was always the possibility of a trade and getting back involved if they felt strongly about a player.

The Knights had drafted 12 players in the 2017 Entry Draft and the majority of them remained in the team's future plans. Certainly the top four picks — Cody Glass, Nick Suzuki, Erik Brannstrom and Nicolas Hague — were making progress in their development, and they were not about to be traded anywhere anytime soon.

Most of the team gathered near the D Las Vegas on June 13 for what was termed a "Stick Salute to Vegas" event. Originally, the team did not want to do anything, but after fans weighed in on social media that they wanted to show their appreciation, the team reconsidered.

"Once we had a chance to step back and really think about how this community supported our franchise every single day, it felt like, 'You know what? We've got to do something'", team president Kerry Bubolz said. "We just put our heads together and started thinking through what that would look like … and we're going to do an official stick salute to our fans."

The temperature was in the triple digits, but more than 7,500 fans showed up to pay tribute to their heroes. McPhee and Gallant were there along with the players. Schmidt told the crowd: "I tell you guys, this is the most fun time I've ever had in my life. All of you are a part of it. These guys behind me, I just wanted to say thank you so much."

Epilogue

With success comes reward. And in the case of the Golden Knights, there were several awards coming the franchise's way, both collectively and individually.

The NHL Awards Show was held at the Hard Rock Hotel in Las Vegas on June 20, and four members of the organization were nominated for awards. Gerard Gallant was one of three finalists for the Jack Adams Award, which goes to the coach of the year and is voted on by the league's broadcasters. George McPhee was a finalist for General Manager of the Year. William Karlsson was a finalist for the Lady Byng Memorial Trophy, which is awarded for gentlemanly play and is voted on by the Professional Hockey Writers Association, and Deryk Engelland was a finalist for the Mark Messier NHL Leadership Award, which goes to the player who shows leadership qualities both on and off the ice.

The Awards Show is televised throughout North America and it's considered to be a big deal. This year, the show would celebrate achievement and reflect back on tragedy. The events of October 1 in Las Vegas were to be recalled, and several survivors and first responders were to be acknowledged. Nick Robone, the assistant coach for UNLV's hockey club who was shot while attending the Route 91 Harvest Music Festival that night, announced that Gallant had won the Adams.

Karlsson, who had just 12 minutes in penalties while amassing a career-best 43 goals and 78 points, won the Lady Byng. Engelland was selected as the Messier recipient and McPhee was named the General Manager of the Year. No one could remember a time when individuals from one team won so many awards in one night.

A month earlier in New York, the Golden Knights organization was selected as the "Sports Team of the Year", by the Sports Business Journal, beating out the Houston Astros of Major League Baseball, the Golden State Warriors and Toronto Raptors of the National Basketball Association, the Nashville Predators of the NHL and Atlanta FC of Major League Soccer.

It was an award that didn't get a lot of notice locally but it was a hint of recognition for the hard work by the team's business, marketing, entertainment and ticketing staffs.

The team's Golden Knights Foundation had raised millions of dollars for charity and had woven itself into the fabric of the community. The Knights' partnership with the Clark County School District to have hockey be part of the physical education curriculum was being enthusiastically received in those middle schools that were participating. The youth hockey program, which the team considers critical to growing the sport and creating that next generation of fans, had made steady growth. According to figures from USA Hockey, Nevada saw a 25 percent increase in participation overall and a 43 percent increase when it came to girls playing youth hockey.

On June 22, the Golden Knights had a full table on the floor at the American Airlines Center for the NHL Draft. McPhee opted not to give up any assets to trade back into the first round, and the Knights spent the following day drafting eight players. Their top pick for 2018 was Ivan Morozov, an 18-year-old center from Russia who the team selected with the 61st overall pick. Morozov, a playmaker and adept passer, caught the eye of Knights' scouts during the Under-18 World Championships, and the team had him rated as a first-round pick. That he was still on the board late in the second round was fortuitous. Time will tell if Morozov pans out.

June 24 was the start of free agency, and players who were unrestricted free agents could begin interviewing with other teams in advance of July 1, the first day a player could sign. The Knights had four UFAs — James Neal, David Perron, Luca Sbisa and Ryan Reaves. McPhee made offers to all four, but the players were entertaining other opportunities. Only Reaves would return for the 2018-19 season as Neal went to Calgary, Perron signed with St. Louis while Sbisa searched for a new NHL team.

"You have to pay attention to the analytics," McPhee said. "They really help you make your decisions now. There's certain things it tells you that you have to pay attention to. It's really different. But it makes things easier.

"Sometimes you feel a certain way about a player, but the information you have tells you something different. Especially now in the cap world, you have to make some cold, hard decisions. We made offers to all of our free agents—every single one. Throughout the year and even this week, there was more discussion with each one, with Perron, with Reaves and with James. We were very comfortable with where we were, and, based on what's transpired, we made very healthy offers. I think we handled that very, very well."

The Knights attempted to make a run at John Tavares, the New York Islanders captain and star center who was the top target among free agents. However, Tavares and his agent, Pat

Brisson, opted not to have a face-to-face meeting with McPhee. San Jose, Dallas, Tampa Bay, Boston and Toronto all met with Tavares and Brisson in Los Angeles along with the Islanders. He would eventually sign with Toronto.

Vegas also was unable to pursue Capitals defenseman John Carlson, who opted to re-sign with Washington for eight years and $64 million. Another free agent, Ilya Kovalchuk, the former New Jersey Devils forward who had spent the last five years playing in Russia, returned to the NHL as he signed with Los Angeles.

They did sign a couple of free agents — center Paul Stastny who was playing for Winnipeg, and defenseman Nick Holden, who was with Boston.

"We had our eye on him for quite a while," McPhee said of Stastny. "He's a really talented, skilled guy. He's a playmaker and you always want playmakers. It's hard for goal scorers to score if they don't have playmakers. He does that. He's a real good person, good solid pro. We do like having centers. You can move centers around the lineup, you can have centers on the wing. You can't get wingers to play center."

As for keeping Reaves, McPhee said: "Ryan is rare in that he's one of those big, physical guys that can play. You can put him anywhere on the ice. Anytime we need him against any other line, you don't get exposed. It's very nice to have that combination of a player — they're hard to find. It's an old expression, but he keeps the flies out of the honey. It's nice to have him around. When we first started with our club, I didn't feel that we needed that because we didn't have stars to protect. As the season got going and progressed, we had some players that turned out to be real good players and some teams were playing us a little harder and a little chippier and thought they were going to get something. We didn't want them getting too overzealous with our players."

McPhee also had his restricted free agents to worry about with William Karlsson at the top of the list. Teams had to make qualifying offers to their RFAs or risk losing them as unrestricted free agents. Sure enough, McPhee gave Karlsson a qualifying offer. He also gave offers to Shea Theodore, Colin Miller, Will Carrier and Tomas Nosek.

Miller signed a four-year, $15.5 million extension on July 7. Nosek signed a one-year deal for $962,500 on July 18, avoiding arbitration as well. Carrier signed a two-year, $1.45 million contract on July 23.

On July 13, the team announced it had signed Marc-Andre Fleury, who had one year remaining on his contract, to a three-year extension worth $21 million. The face of the franchise wasn't going anywhere.

"I guess you guys will be stuck with me for a little bit longer," Fleury said. "I'm really excited about it. My family and I really love Vegas, the organization, my teammates. I feel very blessed to have this opportunity to keep playing in front of you guys for a few more years."

On August 4, with Karlsson's arbitration hearing scheduled for that day, the two sides came to an agreement on a one-year, $5.25 million contract to avoid going in front of the arbiter.

"This is a fair deal and I'm glad it's done. It's a relief and now we can focus on the season ahead," Karlsson said after the bridge deal was announced. "I love playing in Vegas. I couldn't imagine playing anywhere else. I'm hoping we can work out a long-term deal and I'll be here for my whole career."

There was no lack of news off the ice, as the team had announced that it had sold out its season ticket allotment for

2018-19. On July 19, a deal was struck with the United States Army over the trademark dispute regarding "Golden Knights".

"We are pleased that we have agreed to coexist regarding the use of the 'Golden Knights' mark and name," Foley said in a statement. "Our discussions with the Army were collaborative and productive throughout this entire process. We are appreciative of their efforts and commitment to reaching an amicable resolution."

But while one legal issue was settled, the team found itself embroiled in a battle withStubHub, the secondary ticket provider the Knights had used as their official resale outlet. The team claimed StubHub owed it more than $1.2 million from ticket sales during the playoffs.

Back on the ice, 44 players participated in the team's development camp at City National Arena. Among those skating was Gage Quinney, the son of former Las Vegas Thunder star Ken Quinney. Gage, who was a free agent and had been in the Pittsburgh Penguins organization, was born in Las Vegas and he was going to come to training camp in the fall hoping to land a spot on the opening night roster. If he was successful, he would be the first native-born Las Vegan to play in the NHL. Jason Zucker, who grew up in Las Vegas, was born in California.

There wasn't as much time to rest and recover. But that's what happens when you play for the Stanley Cup. And as Gerard Gallant and his staff left town and the players had gone their separate ways, everyone had one eye on the calendar. The 2018-19 NHL schedule was released on June 21, and the Knights would open their second NHL season at home on October 4 against Philadelphia. Fleury wouldn't have to wait as long to go back to Pittsburgh because the Knights were scheduled to face the Penguins October 11. Their first chance to get back at the Capitals would come the night before on October 10 in the nation's capital.

The summer would be brief. But the feeling that came with having accomplished something so remarkable would last with the organization for a lifetime.

Acknowledgements

I would like to thank Herb Jaffe, who took the time to meticulously edit the book and to his wife Fran for her love and support.

I'd also like to thank Angela Hoy and the BookLocker team, particularly Todd Engel, who did an amazing job designing the book jacket. Thanks also to photographer Josh Holmberg, whose photos are on the front cover, and to Craig Campbell of the Hockey Hall of Fame for giving his blessing to use Josh's work.

These kind of projects do not come together without the backing of family and friends. My brothers Mitch and Norm and my sister Barbara have been in my corner from the beginning as have my uncle Mike Birnbaum and my aunts Fran Birnbaum and Susan Tonry. In addition, my niece Melanie Entner and my nephews Michael Entner, Adam Carp and Jordan Esparza and their spouses have been supportive of me and my work.

I also want to thank Ed Graney and his wife Bonnie, along with Ron Kanowski and his wife Linda and Ailene Voisin for their longtime friendship, input and feedback. We've traveled a lot of miles together over the years. I would also like to thank fellow journalist, author, and friend Rob Miech for his believing in me and the book, along with his insight to help getting this to print as well as journalists Helene Elliott, Michael Russo, Kenny Albert and Elliotte Friedman for their endorsements of this project.

Finally, thanks to the Golden Knights' fan base, which extends well beyond Southern Nevada and has been so supportive of having major league professional sports in Las Vegas. This book was written with you in mind. Enjoy!

CPSIA information can be obtained
at www.ICGtesting.com
Printed in the USA
LVHW040243281118
598388LV00014B/442/P